T0338127

Christian Philosophy and Free Will

Other Books of Interest from St. Augustine's Press

Christian Philosophy and Free Will

By Josef Seifert[1]

ST. AUGUSTINE'S PRESS
South Bend, Indiana

Manufactured in the United States of America.

1 2 3 4 5 6   25 24 23 22 21 20 19

Library of Congress Cataloging in Publication Data
Seifert, Josef, 1945–
Christian philosophy and free will / Josef Seifert. –
1st [edition].
pages cm
Includes index.
ISBN 978-1-58731-116-1 (hardcover: alk. paper) 1. Christian philosophy. 2. Free will and determinism. 3. Faith and reason
– Christianity. I. Title.
BR100.S375 2014
190 – dc23   2014009625

∞ The paper used in this publication meets the minimum requirements of the American National Standard for Information Sciences Permanence of Paper for Printed Materials, ANSI Z39.48-1984.

St. Augustine's Press
www.staugustine.net

In vivid memory and veneration of Saint Pope John Paul II
dedicated to all those who love and seek truth,
most especially to those who wish to sore up to the
knowledge of truth on the two wings of fides and ratio
and to all those who question their value or doubt of
their deep unity

"SOAR"

FOREWORD
BY JOHN FINNIS

This book's illuminatingly argued accounts of sound and
unsound understandings of the phrase, and enterprise,
Christian philosophy, and of the reality we call *free will*, are
the latest fruits, for English-speaking readers, of Josef
Seifert's remarkable, fruitful dedication to philosophical
reflection and pedagogy. In years past I had the opportu-
nity of participating, in a small way but more than once,
in his Academy's teaching and debates, and it is a privi-
lege to have the present occasion for commending his
work and works to enquirers interested in either or both
of those two peculiarly important topics. The latter, free
will, concerns most fundamental truths about our nature
and unique place in the world we experience. The former,
Christian philosophy, concerns the most reliable method
and matrix for understanding and right judgment about
those and all other truths accessible to philosophical en-
quiry and methods.

Philosophy can affirm the *possibility* that there are two
lights on reality: philosophy (informed by experience and
the natural and historical sciences) and a historically given
revelation. When pursued resolutely, through to the rational affirmation of Creation by a transcendent intelligence and will, philosophy can, moreover, envisage and
indeed anticipate some communication of information by
that Creative intelligence, communication(s) made by the

Creator's free choice of time(s), place(s) and means. But that such a possibility and anticipation is also a fact, a factual message unfolded—revealed—across the history of Israel, becoming sufficiently intelligible in the life and words of Christ, is not a philosophical truth or discovery. It is, rather, rationally warranted belief in testimony of witnesses of various kinds, at its peak in the testimony of the witnesses to the words and deeds of Jesus of Nazareth. This belief in testimony does not in itself involve a "leap." But the *content* of the message believed conveys not only facts (aspects of, and propositions about, reality) that far exceed what reason working philosophically on the data of experience could anticipate or can securely understand, but also (paradigmatically in the Gospel) includes also, and centrally, an *invitation* to commit oneself to a love of God and neighbor and self that is properly adapted to eternal life in the "household" of the triune God. For it is a central element in the information made available to us only by revelation that a resurrected life, to be lived in God's company after one's death, is offered by divine gift, unmerited but somehow conditional on one's free choice(s) accepting or spurning such divine graciousness. To believe, in the full sense of commitment to this message and this invited conversion of life, does have something of the quality of a leap. Certainly the content of revelation amounts to a "quantum leap" in the body of truths available for reasonable acceptance. The reflective acceptance of all these truths—without incoherence but also without a commingling that would deny or forget their differing sources *quoad nos*, and thus the differing methods for showing them to be warranted—is peculiarly the task and vocation of a Christian philosophy in its clarifying partnership (again without commingling) with a theology faithful to revelation and to the doctrine by which revelation is articulated, guarded and expounded.

The complexity which gives rise to debates, errors, and nuances about Christian philosophy arises not only from this duality of the lights on reality that are available to us, but also (to shift the metaphor) from the fact that Revelation partially *overlaps* with Natural Reason (reason unaided by revelation). For, while large tracts of Revelation and of Natural Reason are peculiar to each and involve no overlap of substantive content, there is a very significant area accessible to *both* these sources of true judgment and belief. The existence of God, the fact of Creation, some aspects of God's nature, and of human nature, and in principle the whole of natural moral law (morality as it binds all human persons independently of revelation): these are prime instances of subject-matter within the overlap. And among the aspects of divine and human nature that are thus knowable both by natural reason and by authentic public revelation (through the prophets and teachers of ancient Israel), the reality of free will is among the very most significant. Human persons of sufficient capacity can and do make some free choices, and philosophical reflection resolutely pursued shows that these choices also be somehow analogous, in their freedom from determination, to the infinitely more sovereign freedom manifested in the divine choice to create *ex nihilo*, and to create *this* universe rather than any other. For: such choices— human and, *mutatis mutandis*, divine—are free in the strong sense that they are determined by nothing, whether inside or outside the acting person, save the choosing itself. In that strong sense, *the reality of free will* is, of course, widely denied by our philosophically inclined but secular and more or less materialist or scientistic contemporaries.

And it is a truth that was—I would say—more clearly and firmly apprehended by the keepers of the Old Covenant than by the keepers of Greece's philosophical flame. On both grounds, it is a subject-matter or thing peculiarly appropriate for exemplifying *both* philosophical method as such *and* a set of sound philosophical positions (further secured by the information afforded by revelation) that we can call an important part of Christian philosophy.

Josef Seifert's twinned essays here, on the character of such philosophy and then, exemplarily, on free will, are works that carefully, thoroughly, and with real penetration offer readers a path to surer knowledge, both of a reality that is truly remarkable (though also palpable and somehow commonplace) and of philosophy's enhanced resources for apprehending that reality and affirming its truth against skeptical doubts, sophisms, and denials.

INTRODUCTION

FREE WILL AND CHRISTIAN PHILOSOPHY[2]

I want to address in the first part of this book two important topics in their inner connection: Christian philosophy and free will.

The question whether there is such a thing as Christian philosophy and if so, what it is, has been the object of hot debates among philosophers, especially in the fourth decade of the last century when both many secular thinkers such as Emile Bréhier, Léon Brunschvicg, Heidegger,[3] and prominent Neo-scholastic philosophers[4] entirely rejected the notion of Christian philosophy as a wooden iron. Now while other thinkers radically, and with strong reasons,[5] rejected this negation of the existence of a "Christian philosophy," they defended very different ideas of "Christian philosophy" and of understanding the relation between human reason and faith.[6] The reason why the task to better understand this question and to throw new light on it is of highest interest for Christian philosophers is obvious.

Our second topic of free will, however, is by no means of lesser interest. Given the importance of the question of free will for ethics, philosophy of man, metaphysics and philosophy of religion, and in view of the many arguments for and against our possessing free will, free will is for any philosopher one of the most exciting themes of philosophical reflection. The theme is of quite particular interest for any Christian philosopher, given the many debates over whether free will is an indispensable condition of the truth of the Christian religion or whether on the contrary the ancient philosophical teaching on human free will is opposed to Christian faith that teaches us the necessity of divine grace, divine sovereignty, omniscience and omnipotence, divine predestination and pre-election, each of which seems to exclude human free will. Thus the topic of free will occupies a central place within what might be called Christian philosophy.

While I shall treat this topic in the second part of this small book, I shall investigate in its first part the question whether Christian philosophy exists and, if so, what it is, defending the view that it exists in different senses and that its negation is a prejudice[7] but that the different notions of "Christian philosophy" should be very clearly analyzed and distinguished. First off, I shall exclude five notions of "Christian philosophy" as either insufficient or mistaken concepts, some of which would even justify the verdict that the notion of "Christian philosophy" is a "wooden iron." This analysis of "what Christian philosophy is not" will be followed by an analysis of an impressive number of eleven acceptable meanings of the notion of "Christian philosophy" that justify the use of this—generally speaking—confused and therefore misleading term by crystallizing and clarifying its correct and even sublime senses. I hope thereby also to shed some light on the historically most important debates on this issue that took place in the 1930s in France, debates in which many of these quite distinct senses of "Christian philosophy" have been confused with each other.[8]

PART I

DOES CHRISTIAN PHILOSOPHY EXIST AND, IF SO, WHAT IS IT?

I. WHAT CHRISTIAN PHILOSOPHY IS NOT (INSUFFICIENT OR MISTAKEN CONCEPTS OF CHRISTIAN PHILOSOPHY)

1. CHRISTIAN PHILOSOPHY AS THE PHILOSOPHY OF A CHRISTIAN?

One might simply define Christian philosophy as the philosophy of a Christian: but as soon as we reflect on this definition, we understand that it does not lead to a meaningful concept of "Christian philosophy," already for the simple fact that not only heterodox Christians or Christians in name only, but also many firmly believing Christians, lamentable as it is, have held all kinds of philosophies, many of which are objectively and logically incompatible with Christian Revelation, such as relativism, skepticism, determinism, Hegelianism, Heideggerianism, etc. Therefore there is no content to such a "philosophy of Christians," for which reason it is also clear that simple adherence to the apostolic or Nicene Creed, if its philosophical implications are not understood, cannot provide a sufficiently sound basis of anything that could rightfully be called a Christian philosophy.[9]

2. CHRISTIAN PHILOSOPHY AS FIDEISM

Christian philosophy can secondly be understood as a philosophy that would presuppose faith in such a way that all its cognitions, at least knowledge of the most basic topics of philosophy, would be gained by us only through divine Revelation through Jesus Christ. Christian philosophy would then be a philosophy that takes the Creed as the exclusive starting point of all its search and acquisition of wisdom. Underlying this notion of Christian philosophy is often a radical philosophical skepticism or a more general notion of the relation between philosophy and religion or world-view that not only distinguishes scientific philosophy from rationally unfounded *Weltanschauung* and *Weltanschaauungsphilosophie*, a view that also Husserl holds,[10] but also insists that all scientific philosophy entirely depends on different pre-theoretical world-views.

In its most radical form, this conception of philosophy amounts to a position that denies any real knowledge of the subject matters of philosophy that would be independent of rationally unjustifiable beliefs. According to the Neo-Calvinist reformed philosophy of Herman Dooyeweerd,[11] William Young,[12] and others there is a difference between *Weltanschauung* and scientific philosophy, but the *Weltanschauung* must not be despised. On the contrary, and wholly against Husserl's view of their relation,[13] rationally ungroundable *Weltanschauung* is the foundation of all philosophy and constitutes the ultimate ground of all its contents. It consists in and embraces philosophically unknowable convictions and foundations. Scientific philosophy then brings as it were this prescientific world view *auf den philosophischen Begriff,* to a more rational self-awareness. Reason is according to this view corrupt, and as soon as it leaves the level of logic and a more formal scientific mode of thinking and turns to concrete contents, it needs to have prescientific foundations, and for the most part has or should at least have religious ones. The answers to questions such as What is truth? What is man? Do we have a soul? Do we have free will? What is moral good and evil? Is theism or atheism true?, etc., could under this assumption only be based on a prescientific faith.

The ideal case of such a relation between philosophy and *Weltanschauung* would be *Christian philosophy* which embraces Christian faith and not an irrational secular *Weltanschauung* as its basis.[14] This notion of "Christian philosophy" corresponds to a radical version of Luther's *sola fide* teaching and has no doubt certain parallels in some Jewish and Islamic thought. This position is quite similar to the "Christian bioethics" of T. H. Engelhardt, Jr., and somewhat close to some passages in Shestov,[15] as well as to some passages in Gilson.[16] I reject this fideistic notion of Christian philosophy on six grounds:

1. It is clearly self-contradictory because its description of philosophy is not at all based on Christian faith but presupposes a philosophical knowledge that includes many elements of logic and other parts of epistemology and views on non-formal subject matters that are *definitely not derived from Revelation* and on which the whole system rests.

2. In actual fact no act of reasonable faith is possible or even conceivable without acts of rational knowledge

that do not depend on faith, wherefore fideism goes against evident truth.

3. While rightly recognizing the strong influence of sinful tendencies and unbelief and the positive influence of virtues and Christian faith on philosophy, fideism completely fails to recognize the proper nature and validity of authentic philosophical methods of knowledge that do not take their starting point in Christian faith which, on the contrary, in a certain sense (that reminds us of the scholastic principle "grace presupposes nature") already presupposes many actually or potentially philosophical insights, but in the nature of things clearly given to human reason.[17]

4. Fideism reduces philosophy to theology and hence in the last analysis denies philosophy, forgetting both the indispensable philosophical foundations of theology and the harmony between faith and reason.

5. Fideism is an utterly ahistorical position given the fact that most of the results of the philosophies of Aristotle, Plato, and other pre-Christian philosophers have been integrated in Christian philosophy such that a large body of contents is common between pagan and Christian philosophers, not to speak of some purely philosophical parts of Sacred Scripture.[18]

6. Last but not least, fideism of this kind denies any rational basis for an intercultural and interreligious dialogue and any basis of such a dialogue and of a pluralistic society and state in a universal natural law written in our hearts[19] and other foundations of truth about God, the world, man and morality, on which alone in a secular and pluralistic society a moral,

political, and national, let alone global, legal order can rest.[20]

3. "CHRISTIAN PHILOSOPHY" AS A "DETERMINATE SCHOOL"

A third deficient notion, I believe, of Christian philosophy is its identification with the philosophy of a particular thinker or school, such as when Christian philosophy / or *philosophia perennis* is explicitly or implicitly identified with Thomism, as in many Catholic, or with Soeren Kierkegaard or with "reformed Calvinist philosophy," as in some protestant circles. Such a virtual identification of Christian philosophy with one specific school fails to take into account the principle of any authentic (Christian) philosophy, a principle formulated by Saint Paul that is incompatible with any identification of *the* truth with *one* school of philosophy only. He writes: "examine everything carefully; hold fast to that which is good."[21] One might express the same principle also by saying *diligere veritatem omnem et in omnibus — love all truth and love it in everything*[22] — a conception of philosophy that looks only for the truth in whoever stated it and is far more akin to the spirit of Saint Thomas himself than a rigid Thomism that does not want to open itself to any insight found outside Thomism let alone to insights critical of some errors in Thomism. This is a sin against Thomas himself who always examines opposite positions and seeks to distill the truth contained in each of them, not in a syncretism or eclecticism, but, by always attempting to go back to things themselves, seeking to unite them in a *corpus veritatis*, wherefore Saint Thomas himself, in contrast to many Thomists, represents the very opposite of this third conception of Christian philosophy.[23]

4. GNOSTIC OR ENLIGHTENED CONCEPTS OF "CHRISTIAN PHILOSOPHY" AS RADICAL REINTERPRETATIONS, DISTORTIONS, AND NEGATIONS OF CHRISTIANITY

Another wrong and far more aberrant Gnostic or "enlightened" notion of "Christian philosophy" is, as it were, the precise opposite of fideism (the second wrong notion of "Christian philosophy"). It presupposes that religion is just something for the masses and that it's higher meaning can only be known by human reason and pure philosophy. According to this concept of Christian philosophy, Christianity properly speaking has at best a symbolic value as a child-like expression of a higher truth which only the deep philosopher, the enlightened or initiated man, understands. This kind of "Christian philosophy" has its roots in Gnosticism which developed during the first centuries of Christianity but reached a certain climax in the German philosophy of the 18th and 19th centuries. Almost all philosophies of religion in German idealism were of this nature, specifically Kant's and Fichte's,[24] Schelling's, and most of all Hegel's, which led him to a radical reinterpretation of Christianity that, however, he himself calls Christian philosophy or a "philosophical taking care of the Christian Religion."[25] The fact that famous Christian theologians, such as the Catholic theologian Karl Rahner, use the Hegelian dialectics and philosophy of religion in their theology of incarnation, in no way renders this philosophy compatible with Christianity. To say, with Rahner's essay on incarnation, that "[w]hen God wants to become non-God, man emerges," applies Hegelian thoughts to theology but has nothing in common with Christianity. First of all, according to the Christian faith, God does not at all cease to be God (which is intrinsically impossible) in incarnation; on the contrary: He remains eternally God but assumed human nature, mysteriously uniting it with His Divine nature; secondly, according to the Christian faith, God does not incarnate in every man but only in the unique God-Man Jesus Christ; thirdly, His motive to become man is His unspeakable love of man and will to redeem Him, and in no way some kind of self-negation, self-cancellation ("Selbstaufhebung") or annihilation of Himself in "wanting to be non-God." We find similar highly Gnostic tendencies also in Michel Henry, considered by many as a prominent Christian philosopher of the twentieth century, and many others.[26] I would say that, under the appearance of Christian philosophy, these philosophies constitute a radical opposite to Christianity, a thesis which applies equally to liberation philosophy and liberation theology, which give to Christian Revelation a purely secular Marxist interpretation.[27]

Against such forms of completely secularized notions of Christian philosophy stands Kierkegaard's anti-Hegelian notion of Christian philosophy or Christian thought that insists very rightly both a) on the total impossibility to reduce the Christian message to a secular ideology or philosophy and b) on the impossibility to demonstrate with pure reason the awe-inspiring and for pure reason paradoxical mysteries of Christian faith. While Kierkegaard seems to be perfectly right on these two points, he seems, however, at times to get close to a fideism (concept 2 of Christian philosophy) rooted in a radical dichotomy between faith and reason, which I consider another and opposite fundamental misconception of Christian philosophy discussed above.[28]

5. "CHRISTIAN PHILOSOPHY" AS A PURELY PHILOSOPHICAL JUSTIFICATION OF THE AUTHENTIC CONTENTS OF THE CHRISTIAN CREED WITHOUT SEEING ANY NEED FOR ANY FAITH OR GRACE TO ADHERE TO DIVINE REVELATION AND CHRIST

A very different notion of "Christian philosophy" is defended by mostly orthodox Christians who believe, however, that they can explain adherence to the Christian Creed in a purely philosophical way that neither needs a supernatural act of faith nor the grace of being drawn by the Father, nor entails mysteries that cannot be believed without a leap of faith that goes beyond all natural philosophical speculations. These Christian philosophers usually share authentic Christian beliefs, without gnostically reinterpreting their contents, and make many interesting and excellent observations in their defense, but they interpret the faith in a somewhat or entirely naturalistic and rationalistic manner.

According to some of them, acceptance of pure and not watered down Christianity would be an act of certain philosophical knowledge. The kind of weight that they give in this context to the empty tomb can of course be understood as a sign of their anti-Bultmannian belief that Christ truly has risen, but frequently they understand it in such a way that any reasonable and rational human person must admit, against all kinds of Bultmannian and subjectivist hermeneutical reinterpretations of the empty tomb, that not only a paranormal event happened and indeed Jesus' tomb was empty but that the empty tomb proves Christ's resurrection.[29] But they forget that however strong reasons[30] we have humanly speaking not to doubt the evangelical accounts of the resurrection and of the empty tomb,[31] the content of our faith in resurrection goes far, far beyond the empty tomb. The real nature and meaning of resurrection *reveals itself* through the empty tomb and other miracles, but the reality of resurrection is far more than the empty tomb itself and unable to be demonstrated by it to an unbelieving spirit. Such Christian philosophers fail at times to see that the essential core of resurrection is a supernatural event that presupposes that God himself became man, assumed a human nature, and through his own divine power was able to rise from the tomb, thereby completing our redemption. These mysteries of the true divinity and rising from the dead of the God-Man can of course in no way be rationally proven or explained by simply giving rational demonstrations of the "empty tomb,"[32] an approach to Christianity that deprives it wholly of its utter mysteriousness and character of "scandal" and "paradox" for natural human reason, as Soeren Kierkegaard and Gabriel Marcel insisted.[33]

Other defenders of this type of Christian philosophy seek to demonstrate or present mysteries of faith as probable to pure reason, either as a knowledge of superior probability and chance of being true than atheism, or only as equally probable as its opposite.[34]

Still other defenders of this type of "Christian philosophy" present Christian faith in the resurrection of Christ and in other contents of the Christian faith not even as assent to the probable but as a mere acceptance of falsifiable hypotheses or as a rational bet we should take.[35] One might indeed, probably wrongly, see in Pascal's famous presentation of a life based on Christian faith as a "bet" such an attempt at a reduction of faith to a rational bet we should all take because in it we can only lose infinitely less and gain infinitely more than in a life based on unbelief.[36]

Some philosophers of this group, not distinguishing belief in the sense of having of a mere opinion from an act of faith, also deny that Christian faith entails an inner certainty specific to the religious act of believing, an act irreducible to any kind of conditional consent or opinion based on a calculus of probabilities or a bet, well as any purely cognitive rational evidence.[37]

I would argue against this kind of Christian philosophy that it reduces the arch-phenomenon of religious faith to an entirely different thing. An act of faith cannot be explained in terms of certain or probable natural knowledge or in terms of mere bets and hypotheses but has an entirely different nature of believing God and his witnesses. Being *an other-person-directed act*,[38] faith is entirely different from just having an opinion. It also possesses a certainty specific to the believing consent of the faithful and entails an unconditional, not purely hypothetic rational, acceptance of such profound mysteries as the incarnation of the Word, mysteries that we can only accept in a faith in something profoundly hidden and even appearing foolish to natural human reason, as Saint Paul puts it.[39]

But if we reject these five kinds of "Christian philosophy," what then are acceptable senses of "Christian philosophy," if any?

II. VALID SENSES OF CHRISTIAN PHILOSOPHY

1. A PHILOSOPHY COMPATIBLE WITH CHRISTIAN REVELATION AND FAITH

That a philosophy be compatible with Christian Revelation and faith is a minimum condition of its being a "Christian philosophy." If Christian Revelation is of divine origin, then every philosophically known truth is "compatible" with Christian faith, because it is evident, in spite of Averroïst's opposite view, that there cannot be a "double truth" such that what is true in philosophy or science may be false in religion and vice versa. For if some truth is divinely revealed, it can never contradict any other truth.

For as there is no double truth, *any true philosophical discovery regarding issues touched upon by Revelation is compatible with Revelation* and hence in this sense "Christian philosophy."[40] At least a few elements of such a true and therefore "Christian philosophy" can be found in any philosophy.[41] If, however, the conflicts between a given philosophy and the Christian faith exceed the points on which they are compatible, we can certainly not call such a philosophy compatible with Christian faith for the sake of just a few points of agreement between them.

Besides, while each truth that any person in the world discovers is compatible with all other truths and therefore, as the Christian believes, with Christian Revelation, the word of Tertullian about the anima naturaliter Christiana and the compatibility of a philosophy with Christian faith implies much more than non-contradictoriness; namely a compatibility on a far higher moral and metaphysical level than a mere formal-logical freedom of contradiction to revealed truth—in other words, much more than the kind of compatibility mathematics or geography has with Christian faith.[42]

While there are some philosophies that contain only some scarce "grains of truth," overshadowed by errors, as for example atheist Marxism and also the philosophy of Friedrich Nietzsche, and therefore can in no sense as a whole be called Christian philosophies or be regarded compatible with Christianity, other philosophies form a coherent whole deeply and largely compatible with Christian faith and embody a kind of *corpus veritatis*.[43]

In spite of such luminous instances, however, it is still extremely hard or impossible to find, in its perfection, a Christian philosophy in this sense of a full compatibility with the faith, i.e., a philosophy that would not contain a number of sentences and theses that would have to be rejected as false or also as being, in their last consequences, incompatible with the faith.[44] Thus in spite of compatibility with Christian faith being an elementary condition of being a Christian philosophy, a philosophy wholly compatible with faith is hard to find and rarely if ever fully met. For any significant philosophical error about important issues such as knowledge, truth, soul, freedom, or God is objectively speaking incompatible with divine Revelation but human philosophy about such matters often gets engaged in constructions and rarely stays entirely free of more or less serious errors. Thus the *philosophia perennis* in its purity as a "system or a sum of truth"[45] compatible with Christian faith is more a transcendent ideal than a historically accomplished reality. To sum up, we can identify this sense of "Christian philosophy" *in its ideal form* simply with the sum total of all knowledge of truth that can be gained by means of human reason through the use of methods of philosophy and that does not only not contradict it but stands in an inner meaningful relation with revealed truth or is necessarily presupposed by it.

Christian philosophy in this first sense nonetheless, despite being in some way a trans-historical ideal that is never fully reached in history, does possess concrete historical embodiments, such as the philosophy of Augustine or Anselm of Canterbury (Aosta), Thomas Aquinas, whose philosophy in its width and breadth and depth occupies a very unique place in the history of Christian philosophy, Duns Scotus's metaphysics and philosophy of the person, Bonaventure's Augustinianism or the realist phenomenology of Edith Stein and Dietrich von Hildebrand, or Karol Wojtyła's personalism. These philosophies can be regarded as true, though imperfect, historical embodiments of Christian philosophy in the first sense.[46]

2. "CHRISTIAN PHILOSOPHY" AS A PHILOSOPHY THAT TREATS THOSE TOPICS THAT ARE MOST RELEVANT FOR CHRISTIAN FAITH

A further very valid sense of Christian philosophy is a philosophy that occupies itself thematically and at a certain depth with those topics which Christian faith proposes to us as the most important ones: God's existence, the human soul and its immortality, good and evil, the foundations of ethics, the nature of the human person, etc.[47] A philosophy that would just focus on some specialized problems of logic, on questions such as what a literary work of art is, etc. would not per se be Christian, if it were not equally concerned with the mentioned issues.

Now most though not all of these topics that Christian faith recommends to us are also shared by Islamic and Jewish religious thinkers such that this is not yet specifically "Christian" about a philosophy.[48] At any rate, and far more important: Christians who are philosophers should not allow secular philosophers to dictate to them the topics they ought or ought not to investigate, and they should not allow the relativistic and historicist *Zeitgeist* to confine them to treating these centrally important topics in a purely historical way instead of searching for the truth precisely about these things themselves.

3. CHRISTIAN PHILOSOPHY AS AN AUTHENTIC PHILOSOPHY RELYING ON TWO LIGHTS AND AIDED BY THE LIGHT OF FAITH

Another sense of "Christian philosophy" implies that the authentic philosophy and work of natural reason of a person who also accepts the light of divine Revelation will ceteris paribus (supposing equal intelligence, talent, training, invested effort, etc.) be better able to reach the truth than the philosophy of a non-believer.[49] For before the mind of a philosopher who can count on divine Revelation, one and the same reality lies open, illumined not only by the light of reason but also by a second and stronger light of divine Revelation. And as this light partly illuminates the same realities,[50] natural philosophical reason can see better than the non-believer also that part of reality that was in principle open to it already before receiving the second light. Bonaventure explains this through a beautiful image that I interpret here a bit freely,[51] and that undoubtedly incorporates some traces of Plato's image of the cave.[52] Imagine a man who sees a forest only by means of the light of a little fire or of the moon. He will frequently see only contours and shadows and be unable to see the objects distinctly. If, however, the sun illumines the same forest, then the man will not only see more in the daylight when he looks at the same reality he looked at before but now that he has once seen it illumined by the brighter light of the sun, he will also thereafter see the same objects better during the night in the weak light of the moon or of a fire. Even this light will now suffice for the man who once has seen the world in the sunlight to recognize the same objects also clearly in the dimmer light of fire or of the moon from their contours and shadows. While he mistook before certain things for other things and while the moon did not suffice him before to recognize them clearly, he now distinguishes them clearly even when looking upon them in the moonshine or the shimmer of a small fire.

In a similar way, it is far easier for a philosopher to see things in their true nature and avoid errors once he has received an incomparably farther reaching knowledge of them through a divine word. Christian philosophy would then be that better and more adequate philosophy that perceives things that can also be known by natural reason and prior to Revelation because he has seen these same things also through the superior and additional light of faith. This might be applied to the knowledge of the soul, of free will, of the meaning of the human body, of many other things and above all of God and his personhood.[53]

Other examples of more general metaphysical data that do neither for their existence nor for their knowledge *necessarily* presuppose Christian faith, but *de facto* had not been clearly recognized before the divine Revelation of the Old or also of the New Testament, even though this had been possible, fall under this category: for example the creation of the world from nothing, the nature of sin as an offence of God, at least in their full extent, and "an awareness of the metaphysical problem of the person,"[54] at least in her full depth and extent that was discovered in a completely new way under the inspiration of and reflection on the doctrines and mysteries of incarnation and the Holy Trinity.[55]

The decisive point in this conception is that philosophy remains fully philosophy; what it sees, it sees with the light of natural reason and not because of the philosopher's faith. But his reason sees better by having perceived its objects in God's light in their entirety and also regarding those aspects that are hidden to natural reason, and by having seen other, and the most profound, parts of the whole of reality that are complementary to the world as given to human reason.

Of course, this wholesome effect of divine Revelation on philosophical reason will only apply if the faithful is not lazy and if he does not rely on the light of faith to such an extent that he neglects making any serious effort to use his reason, in which case his faith coupled with his laziness of mind can make him a worse philosopher than he was before faith awakened in him, even though he be now far more rooted in the truth than before.

To understand Christian philosophy in this sense preserves the complete distinction between knowledge based on the pure use of natural reason and knowledge by faith but recognizes a profound inner relation between them: the light of faith strengthens the light of reason.[56] This is no doubt a correct and a most important sense of Christian philosophy.

4. CHRISTIAN PHILOSOPHY AS A PHILOSOPHY OF MINDS THAT ARE PURIFIED BY CHRISTIAN VIRTUES TO PERCEIVE TRUTH BETTER

There is a closely related but still very different understanding of Christian philosophy as a philosophy purified and refined by Christian virtues. One might note that philosophy quite generally speaking is not a neutral knowledge such as geographic and mathematical knowledge that is neutral in the sense that it hardly depends on attitudes of the geographer or mathematician, but just on his intellectual depth and talent, studies, and memory. In contrast, philosophical knowledge is profoundly influenced by virtues that open the intellect to truth and on vices of a philosopher that close his mind to truth, blinding it, as Socrates and Plato have so clearly noticed.[57] A Christian philosophy in this sense in its ideal form is the philosophy of a Saint whose love of truth, love of God, humility and profound openness to truth, and whose ardent search for the philosophical truths about the most important subjects enable him or her to a philosophical purity and depth of mind that a person of lesser virtue fails to possess.

More than that, even if a person possesses those sublime virtues that we find in a Socrates or Plato, or also in Epictetus, these purify the mind much less than the specifically and irreducibly Christian virtues.[58] This sense of "Christian philosophy" presupposes not only the Christian faith but also the possession of those new and specifically Christian virtues that do not find sufficient motivation outside the orbit of Christian Revelation.[59] This fourth valid sense of Christian philosophy then is a moral-spiritual one with objective consequences for the quality of purely intellectual philosophical knowledge. It does not per se concern the object of philosophical knowledge but the conditions of the depth and purity of the act of philosophical knowledge in the philosopher-subject.

5. CHRISTIAN PHILOSOPHY AS PHILOSOPHICAL REFLECTION ON THE PHILOSOPHICAL IMPLICATIONS AND PRESUPPOSITIONS OF THE CHRISTIAN FAITH

Other dimensions of Christian philosophy touch the philosophical reflection on philosophical implications and presuppositions of the Christian faith. For example, I will try to show that a great Christian mind such as Calvin or Luther entirely misconceived the objective presupposedness of human and angelic free will, whose necessary presupposedness for the Christian faith I shall investigate in this book.[60]

This reflection does not presuppose the Christian faith nor the possession of particular virtues, and an atheist or non-Christian can very well write this chapter of Christian philosophy. In contrast, a genuine Christian believer may *totally misinterpret* these objective philosophical presuppositions of Christian faith.[61] Thus the atheist can be a far better Christian philosopher in this particular sense of the term than a great Christian thinker who denies human, angelic or divine freedom but nonetheless can be a firm Christian believer, at least as long as he does not understand the objective consequences of his denial of free will. If he understood these, he could, upon denying free will, not remain a Christian believer in any sense of the term.

6. CHRISTIAN PHILOSOPHY AS ESSENTIAL PART OF CHRISTIAN APOLOGETICS —THE PARTIAL TRUTH IN THE FOURTH FALSE CONCEPTION OF CHRISTIAN PHILOSOPHY

As we have seen, any attempt to give a rational demonstration of the revealed truth of Christ's incarnation, passion, and resurrection fails. This does not exclude, however, that philosophy can and should investigate the rationality of the act of faith, the notion and possibility of the miracles reported in the Gospel, and in this way uncover the metaphysical and anthropological plausibility of divine Revelation.

Indeed, for Christian Apologetics—apart from relying on historical, psychological, theological, and other natural human knowledge—philosophical knowledge is of a singular importance in the service of leading truth-seeking persons towards the threshold of a faith that requires, however, a great leap above and beyond all understandable reasons for faith. Even the study of this "more of faith," its recognizing and simultaneously going beyond the limits of pure reason, as well as the rationality of taking this leap of the act of faith and its reasonable grounds, is an important topic of Christian philosophy.

7. CHRISTIAN PHILOSOPHY AS AN ANALYSIS OF THE RATIONALLY GIVEN NECESSARY ESSENCES OF SPECIFICALLY CHRISTIAN RELIGIOUS PHENOMENA, ABOVE ALL OF THE PHENOMENON OF THE HOLY AS EMBODIED IN CHRIST HIMSELF AND IN THE CHRISTIAN VIRTUES

There is a further, closely related and possibly most profound dimension of Christian philosophy and of Christian apologetics, which again does not presuppose that the philosopher is a Christian believer himself but quite the reverse can lead the person, particularly the philosopher, to become a Christian. It played a decisive role in the first or second conversions of Max Scheler, Edith Stein, Dietrich von Hildebrand and others.[62] I refer here to the understanding of the uninventable beauty and perfection of Christ's virtue and holiness and of the specifically Christian virtues and of many other contents of the moral and religious sphere of the Christian religion. All of these, even though they presuppose Christian Revelation for their real existence, can be understood in their true and highly intelligible, even necessary essence by the philosopher, whether he is himself a Christian or not. For example, the descending, merciful love of God, the love of the highest and infinitely perfect being for the lowest sinner, entails a revolution and inner transformation of the ancient concept of love and is, and motivates, an entirely new and evidently more perfect kind of love: *caritas*. Max Scheler showed how the Greek idea of the love of God and of the love of man underwent a radical "change of direction" in Christian religion: instead of God being unable to love creatures and just being the object of the love of all creatures whom he attracts wJÀ ejrovmenoÀ (as the beloved), as Plato and Aristotle believed, now God is not only Love in Himself but bends down to creatures and loves them first (to the point of his passion and death on the Cross). The new reality, degree and immensity of this descending divine love, used by Christ in his conversation with Nicodemus to summarize the whole Gospel,[63] is wholly unheard of in the Islam, and by far exceeds what Jewish faith confesses, even though such a supreme descending love is announced in the prophecies of the Messiah in Isaiah and other prophets.

Now a decisive point to understand here is this: Even though faith in what Christians believe about God and neighbor is presupposed for the birth of *caritas* in the human person, the fruit and essence of this new kind of love and of its metaphysical and religious preconditions and superior moral perfection are accessible to human reason and can be analyzed by rigorous phenomenological analyses.

All the mentioned and countless other things about specifically Christian virtues and about the new spirit of the specifically Christian love of *caritas* can be known by the philosopher and the insight into their essence and moral superiority over the pagan virtues may even constitute a major reason for faith.[64] Christian philosophy in this sense is entirely determined by its object: the essence of specifically Christian phenomena.[65] A methodic foundation of how it is possible to grasp in purely philosophical knowledge the necessary essences of virtues and other religious phenomena, whose attainment presupposes Christian faith but whose essence and sublimity can be understood by any philosopher, believing or not, through pure means of philosophical knowledge, has no doubt, though so magnificently represented by many previous thinkers,[66] reached a new level of clarity within realist phenomenology.[67]

Seeing the sublimity, beauty and superior moral value of these specifically Christian virtues turned into a strong reason for many conversions based on this understanding: a religious faith that raises the human being morally to an incomparably higher level of perfection and saintliness cannot be false because it manifests the rays of the uninventible divine light and holiness![68]

Other such phenomena include Christ himself, the idea of incarnation, redemption, etc.[69]

8. CHRISTIAN PHILOSOPHY UNDERSTOOD AS FULFILLMENT OF THE PHILOSOPHICAL QUEST FOR WISDOM IN CHRISTIAN FAITH ITSELF

Another valid notion of Christian philosophy is reflected in the words of St. Clement of Alexandria that he became a philosopher when he found Christ, or in the Church Father's notion of Christ as supreme philosopher.[70] Here the truth revealed by God being the highest wisdom is seen as fulfilling all human and philosophical aspiration to wisdom, and hence the truest philosopher is the Christian believer. Hence philosophy as the purely human quest for truth by means of our *ratio* is merely a propaedeutic to faith, and hence also a propaedeutic to the truest philosophy which a person only achieves by embracing the Christian faith and through it the supernaturally revealed wisdom of God.[71]

This notion of Christian *philosophy* retains solely the innermost aspect and essential characteristic of the philosopher, that of the quest for wisdom and the wisdom itself that is the object of this quest, leaving entirely out of consideration the question whether this wisdom is sought and gained by the use of innate human cognitive powers or by the gift of divine Revelation and faith. And as the search for wisdom is a deeper essential trait of philosophy than the pursuit of it by means of the mere powers of natural reason, we can consider this a valid and profound sense of Christian philosophy although it abandons a trait that we ordinarily understand to be essential for philosophy: namely that its methods and principles are accessible to natural human reason and do not require faith, wherefore this meaning of Christian philosophy employs a very different sense of the term "philosophy."

9. PHILOSOPHY ABANDONING PARTLY ITS ROLE AS SUPREME HUMAN WISDOM AND "CHRISTIAN PHILOSOPHY" AS A PHILOSOPHY THAT STANDS OPEN TO CORRECTION AND TO COMPLETION BY DIVINE REVELATION: HETERONOMY OF PHILOSOPHY?

Christian philosophy can further be conceived as a philosophy that has an entirely different relation to religion than ancient philosophy.[72] Ancient philosophy assigned to human metaphysical knowledge, under the verdict of whose discovery of eternal truths also religion stands, a higher rank than the Greek religious teachings could rightfully claim. For example Xenophanes and Plato (in Book II of the *Republic*) quite rightly criticized and rejected many aspects and superstitions of (ancient Greek) religion.[73] In the light of Christian religion, the basic relation of philosophy to religion changes drastically. Instead of criticizing religion in the light of philosophical truths, the philosophy of Christians subjects itself freely to its potential correction through Divine Revelation and Church Teaching.

This applies especially, and in some sense *only*,[74] whenever we do not deal with insights into necessary states of affairs known with indubitable certainty, but with philosophical speculations and theories of a far lesser certainty. In these areas Christian thinkers give to the authority of the self-revealing God a far higher rank than to uncertain purely human speculations. However, its old role of judging religions as false remains preserved to this date whenever a philosopher who is a Christian detects an inner contradiction or an obvious deviation from evident truth in certain forms of Christian faith-communities and Creeds. For example, we shall see that any Christian confession that denies human or divine free will must be judged false on purely philosophical grounds.

While one can see a first formulation of this openness of philosophy to a higher divinely revealed wisdom or a *divine word* in Plato's *Phaedo* and in Jewish and other religiously open philosophers, this openness towards mysteries and to a wisdom beyond human wisdom is no doubt specifically characteristic for Christian philosophy.[75]

10. CHRISTIAN PHILOSOPHY AS A SYMBIOSIS OF FAITH AND REASON AND THE NEW CONCEPT OF PHILOSOPHY BECOMING PART OF ONE COMPREHENSIVE WISDOM REACHED BY REASON AND FAITH—THE IDEA OF THE "SUMMA"

Another and not unrelated sense of Christian philosophy can be seen in any thought and work in which philosophical and religious/theological insights are mixed and in no way contained in separation from each other.[76]

The philosophy of Christians, from the Fathers on, in a movement that culminated in the ideal of the philosophical-theological *Summa*, has an entirely different relation to Christian religion than philosophy can have to other, particularly to ancient Greek and Roman religions that are not founded on divine Revelation and do not even make a claim to derive from divine Revelation and whose truth claims philosophers could not simply accept as divinely revealed truth and many of whose evidently false teachings they had to reject vehemently.[77] Christian Philosophers, in contrast, philosophize in a world formed by a religion that they no longer consider to be full of errors, as Plato and the Church Fathers considered, with excellent reasons, Greek religion to be, but as the highest embodiment of superhuman, divine wisdom. Therefore Christian philosophy feels that its deepest perfection lies in being an *ancilla*, a servant to theology, a notion that would require much more precision and must not be understood as abandoning its rightful autonomy and sovereignty as ultimate judge of those eternal truths open to it that allow also the Christian philosopher to reject certain misinterpretations of Christian faith and Holy Scripture as being contrary to reason. The profoundly different relation of philosophy to religion goes hand in hand with a new Socratic wisdom of Christian philosophers: namely that human reason and philosophy cannot know the whole truth and that some of the most profound mysteries of being are inaccessible to it, such as whether man needs redemption in order to reach his natural goal of a blessed eternal life or is destined to a higher supernatural eternal life.

Therefore human reason, according to this Christian wisdom, can find fulfillment of its aspiration to wisdom only in faith in the Word of God made man and through the Holy Spirit who teaches us the truth Christ announced to us. The form in which philosophy exists therefore in the middle ages is as a mere part of a Summa of all wisdom, the most profound parts of which had to be revealed to us by God and have to be believed by us. Instead of feeling the primary call to free religion of its errors about God and man, a call it still retains in relationship to heresies and perversions of Christian religion, Christian philosophy bows humbly its head before the higher wisdom of God and accepts the supernaturally revealed wisdom of God.

11. CHRISTIAN PHILOSOPHY AS A PHILOSOPHY THAT ABANDONS THE SUPERHUMAN TASK OF SHOWING MANKIND THE WAY TO REDEMPTION, OF BEING *ERLÖSUNGSPHILOSOPHIE* AS PLATO'S PHILOSOPHY

Christian philosophy then is also a philosophy that abandons its ultimately unseemly and superhuman aspiration of showing mankind on its own strength the path to purification and redemption, a role, however, in which it might in some sense have truly partaken in ancient Greece, but which, according to the Christian philosopher, ultimately is only that of the Revelation of divine wisdom and a divine redeemer.[78] But the Christian philosopher humbly receives in faith the gift of divine redemption in the wisest act of faith in which human wisdom transcends itself and goes beyond all human wisdom, recognizing that not it, but only Christ can give mankind the gift of redemption and only God can purify us and provide a true *catharsis* from our sins, not philosophy.

Part II

How Is Philosophy of Free Will a Topic of Christian Philosophy? Why Nothing Is Left of Jewish Christian Faith If We Are Not Free?

The example of a philosophy of free will could illustrate each of the very different senses of "Christian philosophy" we distinguished, but I wish to concentrate in the following on just one, the fifth, of the eleven valid senses of Christian philosophy, namely a "Christian philosophy" in the form of a philosophical reflection on the philosophical implications and presuppositions of Christian faith. This reflection is of a purely philosophical nature, entirely based on insights into essentially necessary connections between the objects of Christian faith and free will, and does not presuppose the Christian faith, and therefore can be treated by a non-Christian or even an atheist philosopher much better that by many genuine Christian believers who fail to recognize the philosophical presuppositions and implications of Christian faith. In which ways then do divine Revelation and Christian faith presuppose freedom of will?

1. Without Acknowledging Freedom of the Created Person, God Would Be the Origin of All Evils and Thus a Hyper-Demonic Being

Each metaphysics that denies the free will of humans and of angels, and more precisely the abuse of the immense gift of free will, as source and first cause of all the manifold evils that obviously exist in the world, blames these evils on God or, if he is an atheist, on an unfree natural cause. In either of these two cases, moral evil would evidently not exist at all in the world. For if humans and angels were determined to be evil by a cause extrinsic to themselves, they would be innocent like lambs or, better said, they would be free of guilt like puppets that cannot be guilty of any of the crimes the puppeteer performs with them on a stage. God, however, as long as his existence is not altogether denied, as the source of all evil and suffering, of all holocausts and crimes, would be himself evil. Therefore each denying of human and angelic freedom either leads to atheism or to a polytheism that populates the world with good and evil deities, or to a transformation of God into a super-demon—infinitely more terrible than Satan, because all evils from the beginning to the end of the world would be God's fault alone, which cannot be said of Satan. In contrast to Satan's limited causal role regarding other evils besides his own – if man and angels were not free and if therefore, granted his existence, God had brought into the world all meanness, all lies, all adulteries, all perjuries, rapes, murders, thefts, tortures, hate and envy, genocides and other crimes (including Satan's and his angels' sins) or if He had determined angels and humans to commit them, He would be the only ultimate source of evil (which cannot be said of Lucifer). One cannot imagine a more terrible destruction of the idea of God. God would be an Anti-God. In this case, Ivan Karamazov's rebellion against God as responsible for all evils and his resulting ethically motivated atheism, so powerfully described by Fodor Dostoyevsky in the conversation between Ivan and Alyosha in *The Brothers Karamazov*, would be wholly justified.

2. WITHOUT DIVINE FREEDOM THERE COULD NOT BE ANY CONTINGENT WORLD AND PARTICULARLY NO CREATED FREE PERSON

Parmenides saw deeply that a contingent and temporal world cannot proceed from God by a necessity rooted in the eternal and necessary divine nature and he is completely right that if, as he assumes, the eternal and necessary being could bring forth something only by a necessary and eternal action, non-necessary and temporal beings could not exist in the world and hence the world would have to be a pure illusion.

We may add that, in particular, created free agents could not be explained without creation being a free act of God, because never could unfree causes in nature or in God explain the wonder of free will in finite beings. Even more evidently than contingent beings in the world cannot exist in virtue of a necessary act but only of a free creation through an eternal being, agents endowed with free will in the world can come into being only from a free act of the absolute person.

Therefore, if God were not free, neither the contingent (non-necessarily existent) world nor free agents in it could exist. Therefore, to deny God's freedom of choice, still retaining His existence, will lead to some form of pantheism that dissolves human personhood and freedom, a consequence drawn in many Gnostic, Spinozean, Hegelian and other pantheistic systems. Moreover, if the world and even evil were to flow necessarily from God, God would as well, if not freely, so necessarily, become the cause of evil, as Schelling suggests in his thesis that everything flows with absolute necessity (at least moral necessity) from God.[79] His position against divine free will objectively denies any real creation and conceives of the world as well as of any evils in it as a direct and necessary consequence of divine nature even though, in spite of expressing this deterministic position clearly enough, Schelling does not wish to draw this conclusion in its whole metaphysically devastating force, thus contradicting himself.[80]

3. WITHOUT DIVINE FREEDOM THERE WOULD ALSO BE NO DIVINE HOLINESS

Each adequate idea of God implies His freedom also for another reason: as the condition and origin of His justice, mercy, and holiness that constitute the highest perfection of the person qua person.[81] Without God's supremely perfect freedom the core of divine perfection would be null. God would no longer be just, merciful and holy, and hence not God. To see this one needs to see also that these moral perfections are not restricted to human persons but, as pure perfections, culminate in God's infinite perfection, which not to have seen but having relegated moral virtues to a purely innerworldly human sphere constitutes one of the gravest errors of Aristotle's philosophical theology.[82]

4. BY DENYING DIVINE, ANGELIC, AND HUMAN FREE WILL THE ENTIRE JUDEO-CHRISTIAN REVELATION ABOUT GOD WOULD BE DENIED AND ALL ANTHROPOLOGICAL CONTENTS AND TEACHINGS OF SACRED SCRIPTURE AND

OF THE CHURCH WOULD LOSE THEIR FOUNDATION AND HOLY SCRIPTURE ITSELF WOULD BE RENDERED A WORTHLESS BOOK OF LIES AND STUPIDITY

Without divine free choice, God would not be our creator, nor our redeemer, nor would there exist any reason for gratitude towards God for our creation, nor would there be any sense whatsoever in redemption or in divine forgiveness of sins, because if all of these were not works of divine free choice, they would be nothing.

We would not be creatures but some moments in a necessarily self-unfolding life of God and hence would lose our freedom also in consequence of the inner necessity with which the world would flow from God. Not only by denying human freedom directly but also in consequence of denying divine freedom of choice, as our being and all our actions would be necessary effects of God, there would be no original sin, no personal sin, no redemption from them, no meaning of the divine commandments, nor would any of the divine promises to the just be less than deception. If that were true, also the Sermon on the Mount and the call to holiness would not have any sense any more, let alone eternal reward or punishment. Thus also the Bible would be nonsensical gibberish.[83]

In a word: without free will no Christianity! And also no Judaism and no Islam which recognize many of the mentioned truths about God and man!

Therefore hardly any other naturally knowable truth is more important, not only for the metaphysics of the human person and our personal life, but also for the Christian and any other theistic faith, than this one: that the person, whether human and finite or divine and infinite, possesses free will. This explains as well how the two topics of the present book, the nature of Christian philosophy and a philosophy of freedom of will, are intimately connected.

But at this point we may say: yes, you have given convincing reasons why Christian Revelation and Christian faith necessarily presuppose the existence of free will. But does not precisely this fact prove both Christian faith and the assumption of free will to be illusions? Has not modern brain science proven that free will is an illusion, and with this shown that Christian faith is an illusion as well? Or can you offer any evidence that we do in fact possess free will? If not, all you have shown regarding free will and Christian philosophy is that both are inseparable ideas—but you have not shown that they are more than inseparably connected illusions. We shall attempt to answer this crucial question about the actual existence of human free will in the third part of this book.

PART III

DO WE ACTUALLY POSSESS FREE WILL? –

IN DEFENSE OF FREE WILL[84]

According to the neurobiologist Benjamin Libet, we are incapable of positive free voluntary acts; these, or rather, their mere conscious semblance, are, according to his view, sheer effects of cerebral causes. Notwithstanding this, free will is not impossible; it can exist in the form of "negative free will," that is, of a veto of voluntary movements. Libet states his position in the following manner:

> I have taken an experimental approach to the question of whether we have free will. Freely voluntary acts are preceded by a specific electrical change in the brain (the "readiness potential," RP) that begins 550 msec. before the act. Human subjects became aware of intention to act 350–400 msec. after RP starts, but 200 msec. before the motor act. The volitional process is therefore initiated unconsciously. But the conscious function could still control the outcome; it can veto the act. Free will is therefore not excluded.[85]

In spite of his "experimental approach to the question of whether we have free will," Libet's theses are primarily philosophical ones: the notion of free will, the distinction of "positive voluntary actions" from a vetoing or controlling power of free will, and many others cannot be known by empirical tests per se, but only by philosophical reflection on their outcome and by properly philosophical methods of knowledge.[86]

Given their fundamentally philosophical character, there are many ways in which philosophy can tackle the issues and claims Libet raises in organizing and interpreting his famous tests with free will that result in his denial that we possess positive free will and in his simultaneous claim that we do or at least might possess "negative free will," namely a free veto power.[87]

One of these ways consists in simply asking whether we have cognitive evidence of possessing positive free will. If we can find, as I intend to show in this part of the book, that there is not just one but there are, rather, various ways by which we can gain evident knowledge about human persons' possessing both "positive" and "negative" free will, and if this evidence is sound and founded on rational cognitions of things themselves, Libet's attack on positive free will is thereby refuted. In other words, if we can substantiate authentic philosophical evidences that we possess "positive free will," we will refute, in the strongest possible way, its merely hypothetical denial by Libet; for no matter what way we have to answer his objections and reflect on his test results in detail, a cogent refutation of his hypothetical objections will be guaranteed by the knowledge that we indeed possess free will, a knowledge we can gain, I shall seek to show in the following, along different routes. Thus, abstracting from Libet's experiments, which he himself believes to allow only for hypothetical conclusions, and focusing on purely philosophical evidence for free will that is not merely hypothetical and therefore surpasses in evidence all his merely empirical and at best probable theories, is a perfectly legitimate form of criticism against Libet and is the main purpose of the following reflections.

Following the attempt to complete this primary task of the present analysis, we will also analyze the various meanings of the distinction between positive and negative free will that Libet introduces and show that asserting the one while denying the other entails a logical contradiction.

When we speak of a free act, we mean first that a given act is caused by the person himself who possesses the power of free will, and not by any material or spiritual cause outside of him, neither by chains of electrical and chemical causes in the brain, nor by society and education, nor by God, who would predetermine and force—or determine in a softer way without experienced coercion—a person to act in a certain manner. The person himself as cause of free acts refers, furthermore, to the person as conscious agent who engenders a free act consciously through an inner "fiat" (which is not to deny that the originally conscious act can give rise to different senses of super-conscious or also subconscious will, of which we do not always have conscious, let alone reflexive, awareness). To say that the person causes a free act, therefore, not only excludes that his free acts have a sufficient cause outside of him, but also prohibits that the cause of a free act could be situated in his pre-given nature or his physiological or chemical-electrical makeup or the "unconscious brain," over which he has no dominion and control; in other words, calling a person's will free means, among many other things, that he can determine himself to will, causes his free acts consciously from himself, and is himself lord over his willing or not willing, over the being or non-being of his acts, as Aristotle formulates in a most impressive metaphysical characterization of free will.[88]

Thus, we understand in this work free will in the sense which is often called today, in some abuse of language, "libertarian." Using this term here, we disassociate ourselves from many elements of this view as it is defended by some analytic philosophers and philosophical circles, but do retain its essential tenet that we are, in a sense, the prime mover of our will, its ultimate or first cause, and that it, therefore, truly is up to us what we will or do.[89]

Any compatibilist view that seeks to reconcile determinism with free will believes that, in view of philosophy and science, free will can only be affirmed while simultaneously denying that a truly free subject exists and is the ultimate cause of his acts. According to this view, the experienced free will that does correspond to our feeling to be in command of our actions and is indeed true, inasmuch as we are free from coercion, must in the last analysis be traced back to other causes on which it not only would depend as on conditions or aids but which would determine its content. Such a position, however, basically denies free will and declares it to be an illusion; for, according to this view, the acts that we call free would, in actual fact, be caused and, in their content, determined by causes different from the free subject himself.

Such a view on the compatibility of free will and determinism must be sharply distinguished from a position that only asserts the compatibility between the free will of the contingent free act and its dependence on brain and other *conditions* without which we cannot perform free acts—which are *sine qua nons* but not causes of free acts—

as well as from the compatibility of human free will with a Creator's rendering this will possible, causing our faculty of free will and giving the power of free choice being, manifold support, and incomparably higher value when free will is used for the good, without ever determining the content of our use of free will from without.[90]

Perhaps the compatibilist view has one root in the immensity and therefore incomprehensibility of what we say if we seriously state that the human person possesses free will, which appears to be something too great to attribute to human beings. Do we truly possess free will and does this indeed involve the lordship over the being or non-being of our acts, as Aristotle holds? Is it not a prerogative of God to be Lord over the being or the non-being of something by a simple inner word or *fiat*, without such a *fiat* being determined by any cause other than the person himself in virtue of his free center over which he has sovereign control? Had we therefore not better assume that we are, after all, in the last analysis, determined by brain functions, upbringing, education, role-models, historical circumstances, and so on, or at least by divine pre-determination? Or is there really such a godlike quality in the finite person as to enable him to take an adequate or inadequate stance toward values and things, speaking a free "yes" or "no" to them, therein and thereby becoming the lord over the being and non-being of his acts? Can man verily initiate a new causal chain?[91]

The question whether human free will actually exists is wholly different from the question of what free will is, namely, the question of the essence of free will. The difference that obtains between the two questions is evident when we consider that the denier of human free will must understand the nature of what he denies; moreover, it is quite possible and not contradictory that somebody who understands the essence of free will exactly as we do, ascribes existing free will only to God and denies it of man. Our question in this part of the book is: Does human free will actually exist, and if so, how can we know this?

In order to answer this question, one has to presuppose some knowledge of the essence of free will, the existence of which one discusses, but we shall not treat this question here except (i) to the extent that we have already dealt with it, and (ii) to the extent that the seven ways to know that we possess, in fact, free will simultaneously reveal something about the nature of human free will. Instead, we will build in this short essay on the prephilosophical understanding every man has of the essence of free will and turn right away to the discussion of seven ways in which we can know with certainty that human free will and "positive free will" exist and that we are, in fact, free.

1. A first response taken from the immediate evidence of free will in the cogito imposes itself on us: The power of the free human person over his acts ("for if we will, it is; if we will not, it is not. . .")[92] is given just as immediately as our own existence in the experience of consciously living our being and performing free acts.

We can reach the knowledge of the real existence of our free will in actually experiencing it from within—as part of the indubitable evidence of the *cogito;* it can be known with the same immediacy as our own existence, or in a sense even more immediately, because even if we were mistaken about all other things, it would still be evident to us that we would not want to be deceived, and in this will not to be deceived, we experience our free will with evidence.

The existence of free will thus is, in a certain sense, more primary and indubitable than all other evident truths given in the *Cogito*. Of course, this priority is not to be understood absolutely: for without the evidence of our existence and thinking activity, our freedom and will could not be given. Nevertheless, the remark that our free will is, in a sense, even more evident than our existence is valid *secundum quid* in the following sense: even if we assumed, *per impossibile*, that all other truths given in the *Cogito* would be doubtful, we could still be certain that we freely want and wish to avoid error and to reach the truth. For even if we could be in error about all things, it would still remain true that we do not want to be in error, and of this free will we can have certain knowledge, as Augustine states.[93] While, objectively, the knowledge of the real existence of our free will depends on the evidence of our existence in the *Cogito, sum* and of many other things and states of affairs, the knowledge of the real existence of our free will concretizes the *Cogito, sum* in an extremely significant direction so that we can understand clearly that the evidence of this knowledge somehow exceeds that of any other knowledge and is at least on a par with it.[94]

Thus we may say that nothing is more evident to us than our free will: Our very existence and conscious life are not more indubitably given, though perhaps more easily understood, than our free will. Indeed, we know of our free will with the same type of immediate and thereupon reflective evidence with which we know of our own existence.[95]

Investigating this matter more closely, we could distinguish between the evident givenness of free will on different levels: a) in the immediate inner conscious living of our acts, an intimate inner lived conscious contact with our being;[96] b) at Karol Wojtyła[97] calls "reflective consciousness" (which precedes the fully conscious self-knowledge), c) in explicit reflection and self-knowledge properly speaking, in which we make our personal free will the explicit object of reflection, d) in the insight into the nature of free will, an insight which grasps the necessary and intelligible essence of the person and his free will, which is realized in each and every person, and e) in the clear and indubitable recognition of our personal individual free will, an evident knowledge which depends, on the one hand, on the immediate and reflected experience of our being and free will, and, on the other hand, on the essential insight into the eternal and evident truth of the connection between free will and personhood. The awareness of our own free will—a knowledge which is so evident that it cannot be deception—is, in fact, part of the evidence of the famous *Cogito* of René Descartes[98] and, even more, of the richer and more adequate Augustinian version.[99]

Thus, starting from the immediate self-experience of our conscious life, we gain the evidence that we possess the freedom to will not to err and to will countless other states of affairs, and, in a similar manner, we proceed to the more general evident knowledge of our free will that shows us that we do many things which we would not do if we were not willing and that our willing is if we want it to be and is not if we do not want it to be.[100]

Thus, in all the acts which are implied in our doubt, we have an indubitable experience of our free will to want to know the truth and to will not to be deceived.[101]

The evidence of this knowledge cannot even be refuted by referring to any and all possible forms of experience in which we either are or just feel unfree and mentally paralyzed, or in which, on the contrary, we only feel free, but are in fact manipulated or driven by other causes. The actual partial loss of free will power can be caused indirectly, by reducing the level of our cognitive powers, or directly. The first may occur, for example, through immoderate alcohol consumption that can affect gravely our ability to think clearly, and when we do not clearly understand and think, our free will lacks the knowledge its proper use presupposes. Other causes, for instance consciousness-altering drugs (such as Escopolamina N-Butyl Bromur or Burundanga), may influence our will more directly without suspending necessarily at the same time our thinking capacities, as happens, for instance, after excessive alcohol consumption. Rather, these causes of losing our use of free will through drugs or in consequence of sickly psychological bondages or sexual dependencies on others can produce states of consciousness in which we are passively driven and, even when not losing our intellectual capabilities and all powers of free volition, have a gravely reduced willpower. One may also refer to hypnosis and other similar phenomena which are quite unfit to do the job Wegner attributes to them, namely, to show that free will is an illusion.[102]

In the first place, all, or at least most, of these phenomena imply, or presuppose, already the evidence of our existence and of our real free will, particularly the evidence that we can will not to be deceived or will not to take such drugs as reduce the use of the power of free will or even make us willing-less instruments of the will of others. Secondly, while these phenomena of altered consciousness imply a partial loss of control over our actions, they cannot make us lose our free powers altogether, as for example, the psychiatrist Viktor E. Frankl has shown.[103]

Also, pointing out the undoubtedly great quantity of "idols of self-knowledge" and illusions about one's own acts cannot refute the existence of free will.[104] Invoking possible self-deceptions and cases in which we believe to have acted freely while this was an illusion, in order to prove that free will itself is an illusion, is logically and epistemologically speaking a big mistake: we could not even know what it means that free will is an illusion if our knowledge of what free will itself is or the free will to search the truth and not to be deceived, or the free decision to fight against becoming victims of illusions were itself an illusion. We can here solely briefly sketch the mistakes contained in Wegner's argument against free will and his declaring it an illusion on the basis of the sketched argument:

1) We can never validly infer from "many X's are y" (many experiences of free will are based on a deception or illusion) to "all X's are y" (all experiences of free will and free will itself are an illusion), just as we cannot infer from the fact that many times when we believe to know a truth we are in error: all knowledge of truth could be an error. For, on the contrary, any error necessarily presupposes some knowledge of truth that is not and cannot be an error because, in an error, some true knowledge is presupposed, for example, regarding what an object seems to be or regarding two things which we confuse, but of which we still have some true understanding as condition of the confusion, and so on.[105]

2) Without understanding the nature of free will in what objectively is its essence, and without not falling prey to an illusion in this knowledge, it would make no sense to call free will an illusion.

3) Were a person really not endowed with free will, he

could never be deceived in single cases about having acted freely.

4) Many examples of an alleged lack of free will (for example, of persons carrying out in a fully conscious state—that is, when they are not in the trance of the hypnosis during which they may not be more free than in a dream—orders received while under hypnosis) can easily be explained as not at all entirely eliminating free will, but, instead, as only providing a new motive arising from the unconscious order received in hypnosis to carry out certain morally neutral actions. We must not forget here that the hypnotist has no power over acts that are morally evil and go against the conscience of a person, such as murdering someone (at least after the hypnotized person awakes from narcotic slumber). For example, if I carry out the order I received by a hypnotist who told me under hypnosis: "Normally you go shopping before you pick up your son from school, but today you shall reverse the order," and then I do this, this just means that the unconscious order from the hypnotist gives me an unconscious motive to reverse an entirely neutral order of activities and that this reason to act is stronger than the motive to continue my old habits or routine to do things the other way around. However, this proves neither that the habit that I follow normally nor that the order received in hypnosis suspends my free will; for to accept any conscious and unconscious motive regarding concrete actions still remains a free act and does not eliminate my free decision to pick up my child or to go shopping, which to do in a certain sequence almost requires some irrational reason for following such a neutral sequence, because of the latter's neutrality. That hypnosis does not suspend free will is also obvious from the fact the hypnotist has no power over morally laden decisions, such

as if he ordered me to kill my child on the way home from school, which of course, I am able not to carry out the next day and which hypnosis cannot make me do. Even to let myself be hypnotized is often a free act.

Returning to the Augustinian example of the will not to be deceived, we can recognize its freedom also in another way: the free act of seeking the truth, the intention to get to know it and to avoid living in error, is in no way necessarily in us. We can also take an attitude of indifference towards the truth; we can pursue a life of seeking pleasure without intention to base our personal or moral life on truth. Hence, we experience this will to seek the truth as well as our doubt that is motivated by our will to avoid error (wherefore we ought not to give our consent to judgments rashly), as a free response to an obligation to lead a life based on truth and not to judge irrationally. This free will also presupposes that we cognize the value of truth and of knowledge, as well as the intellectual disvalue of error and the moral disvalue of disregarding truth. In these decisions, our free will is experienced as a freedom of responding to a moral obligation and of taking freely a fundamental good direction of our life towards a life based on truth instead of an irrational or evil one.

Aristotle has formulated this option for or against a life of truth in similarly impressive ways as Augustine, who describes the deeper experience of free will that allows us to choose between two radically different directions of our life in the face of truth, an experience of free will that can be gained even by reflecting on the most radical skeptical doubt.[106]

2. The evidence of our own free will can also be gained through the light of the "eternal truths," namely, necessary and supremely intelligible essences and essentially

necessary states of affairs or "laws": The unique inner perception or grasp—through our intimate conscious contact with our being and life from within—that we really exist and are free to seek or to ignore truth is connected with the light of eternal truths, with insights into necessary essences and states of affairs that are quite independent from our individual person, but without knowledge of which we could not understand the existence of anything.[107] For example, we do not only immediately perceive from within that we live and are conscious, but we understand at the same time the universal truth of the principle of contradiction: "nothing can exist and not exist at the same time and in the same sense," or the general state of affairs seen in the Cogito: Deception and error require the real existence of the person who errs or is deceived; therefore, nobody who errs and is deceived can fail to exist.

As we perceive the concrete fact of our own existence in the light of these eternal truths, so we can also perceive our own free will in the light of the eternal truths about the essence of free will, such as that we cannot will anything of which we do not first have some consciousness and knowledge,[108] or that our will can meaningfully be motivated only if its object is not wholly neutral, but possesses some positive or negative importance, or the insight that we can be motivated by very different kinds of important things: by what is intrinsically good, objectively good for us, or only subjectively satisfying, although neither good in itself nor objectively and truly good for us or for other persons.[109] We have already discussed some other eternal truths about the nature of free will.

Now, we could formulate this second way to know that we possess free will thus: in understanding what free will is, we at the same time perceive in ourselves the actually existing power to act freely. As it were, the light of the insights into universal facts at the same time allows us to understand clearly the instantiation of free will in our own being and conscious life. It is even impossible to separate these two kinds of cognition, a fact which indicates that they mutually imply each other and presuppose each other, though each in a different way: without experiencing our own free will we could not come to understand its essence; and without understanding its timeless essence, we could not become certain that we possess free will.

Thus, while these two kinds of knowledge (of the essence and of the existence of free will) are quite distinct, nevertheless they are deeply intertwined in a twofold way:

1. No one can know the existence of anything without also knowing some universal essential truths about it and, therefore, no one can see clearly that he in fact possesses free will if he does not understand this in the light of the necessary and timeless essence of free will and of its different dimensions.

2. On the other hand, no one can know the universal essence of being or anything else if he does not at the same time know the existence of his act of knowing these things. If he could persistently doubt his own existence and that of his knowledge, he could not know anything with certainty.

In a similar way, although not based on the same clear evidence, one might say that, on the one hand, anyone who understands the nature of free will could not gain this knowledge without the inner experience of his own free will, which discloses to the person simultaneously the nature of free will and the fact that he is free. If man were an unfree animal, he could not understand the essence of free will. On the other hand, nobody could be certain that he is free without gaining some insights into the essence of free will, into what freedom of the will is and what the term means. These remarks might give rise to the suspicion that this argument is circular, which it would be if the same assertion were both a logical conclusion and a premise of a syllogism. But it is not so: rather, two immediate evidences are here so intertwined that none is possible without the other; each depends on the other, but not in the same way nor in the same sense.

3. *The knowledge of free will can also be gained through the mediation of the experience of moral calls and oughts.* This third way to know that we are free can be described thus: we all experience, whenever we experience responsibility or guilt, or blame someone else, that we and each other man ought to do certain things and not to do others. An ought, however, would not only lose any sense without freedom of the will, but, in its experience, freedom is co-given with the same evidence as the ought itself.[110] In a similar way, a call issuing from goods endowed with values to give them their due response, which is, as a matter of fact, the main rational reason for an ought, cannot be perceived without at the same time knowing our free will, without which we could never respond to the call for a due value response.[111]

Therefore, in the experience of any ought or call to give a due response, we are given, with the same evidence with which we know that we ought to do or to omit something, or to perform an inner act due to a beautiful or good object or person, also our free will, which is the only conceivable addressee of an ought or call for a due response, particularly when this ought takes on the character of a moral obligation. No conceivable unfree reaction can ever relate to an ought or to a call from a value *per se*. We can say: nobody can know of an ought or grasp the call to give an adequate response to a good endowed with intrinsic value or an objective good for our own or another person without knowing that he is free; hence, as we do know of many such oughts and calls for a due response, we know that we are free.

The same applies of course to the experience of a "thou ought NOT" . . . to do this or that, or to the experience of bad conscience in which, together with the understanding that we ought not to have done some act, our free will is co-given. To develop this argument further, one would have to defend it against the objection that oughts and values themselves are illusions and that we never truly experience an ought or a call issuing from values to give them a due response.[112]

Against the third way to know our free will from the experience of "oughts" someone might object: we can also give an affective response, that is not within our free power to engender and still is due to a great work of art or to a beloved person; hence to respond to an ought or to a call, or to give a due response, the person and his act need not necessarily be free. To this objection we retort: while it is quite true that a certain kind of adequacy of a response even requires our affections that are not within our free power to engender, and cannot be given as a pure volitional response, which could for example never be the adequate act of compassion with a person who was bereft of a loved one, still also this affective due response that does not stand within our power to engender freely calls for a free sanction, without which our response, as it were, would not enter fully into relation with oughtness and due-ness.[113]

4. *There exists also a fourth kind of argument, a "realist transcendental" proof of "free will as an undeniable truth."* This line of thought argues that any denial of human free will entails a contradiction because its denial entails its assertion or recognition. We may call this an "objectivist transcendental argument" on behalf of our free will because it seeks to demonstrate that everybody who denies free will already presupposes it: Both in the act of denying free will and in insisting that we and everyone else should recognize the truth that there is no free will, we presuppose the evidence that we and other persons are free: only for that reason can we possibly have a moral responsibility towards ourselves and towards others of accepting and of publicizing this alleged truth that there is no free will. Thus, in all of the judgments in which we reject free will, we contradict our deterministic view and presuppose the evidence of free will.[114] For this reason, we can call the existence of human free will an "undeniable truth," because denying it is contradictory and already presupposes it.[115]

A true anecdote told by Hans Jonas helps to illustrate this. At the turn of the 19th century, a group of young physiologists (students of the famous Johannes Müller) met regularly in the house of the physicist Gustav Magnus in Berlin. Two of them (Ernst Brücke and Emil du Bois-Reymond) made a formal pact to spread the truth "that no other forces are at work in the organism except chemical-physical ones." Soon also the young Helmholtz joined them in this solemn pledge. Later, all three men became famous in their fields and remained faithful to their agreement.

The very fact of this pledge, however, already contradicted, without them noticing it, the very content of their promise, or rather, the materialist theory and negation of free will which they pledged to promote throughout their career.[116] For they did not bind themselves, and could not have bound themselves, to leave to the molecules of their brain their respective course of action, because the course of molecular events in their brains, according to their own opinion, was wholly determined since the beginning of the world, nor did they bind themselves by means of their promise to allow these molecules to determine all their speaking and thinking in the future. (This would have been equally senseless for the same reasons.) Rather, they pledged fidelity to their present insight or better, their false opinion. They declared by their pact, at least for themselves, that their person was master over their action. In the very act of making this promise, they trusted something entirely nonphysical, namely, their relationship to what they took to be the truth and their free will to decide over their action. Moreover, they ascribed precisely to this factor a determining power over their brains and bodies—which power, however, had been denied by the content of their thesis. To promise something, with the essentially included conviction to be able to keep such a promise and to be likewise free to break it, this admits a force of free will at work in the organism of man. Faithfulness to one's promise is such a force. Thus, precisely the very "act of vowing always to deny free will and any non-physical force" solemnly confirmed the existence of the very sort of free will and nonphysical forces which they denied!

This argument does not presuppose the flagrant contradiction between a promise to spread determinism but applies analogously to any negation of free will, that is, to any conviction of determinism in which one feels that one ought to accept, to express, let alone to spread or to defend, determinism against the assumption of free will.[117]

5. The evidence of free will can also be obtained by the experience of acts whose objects (persons and their acts) or subjects presuppose and disclose free will. This fifth way to reach the knowledge that human persons possess free will consists in an investigation into the ontological and anthropological conditions of a great number of acts directed at our own or at other persons, and the evidences we have regarding the object and subject of these acts. Thus, not only the other-person-directed acts of vowing or promising mentioned by Jonas, but also the essentially self-directed acts of feeling and experiencing guilt, or of repentance of one's own sins, presuppose free will.[118] In the experience of our guilt and responsibility, as well as in our act of repenting, we find the evidence of our own free will at their root: it would be absolutely senseless to repent of what our nature or brain or society or God compelled us to do.

The experience of our responsibility and of our authentic guilt (distinct from, and presupposed by, mere guilt-complexes), however, not only presupposes but at the same time reveals our free will: the experience of our free will is an essential part of experiencing guilt or repentance. These two experiences are closely related in a unilateral way, in that no one can repent without experiencing responsibility and guilt, and therewith his own freedom (but of course, we can experience our guilt without repenting). We can even experience our guilt and simultaneously explicitly refuse to repent. Mozart's music represents this masterfully in the character of Don Giovanni, who refuses explicitly and repeatedly to repent when the victim of his murder, the father of Donna Anna, appears to him as a ghost in the last act of the opera *Don Giovanni* and urges him to repent.

In a similar way, the essentially other-directed act of gratitude or forgiveness, and many further fundamental human acts directed at other persons presuppose the evidence of freedom, not only in the subject-person, but also in the object-person of these acts. In the act of gratitude, for example, we find that it is rooted in the evidence of the free will of the subject-person (while a feeling of gratitude that is not within our free power to engender is a fundamental human datum, a forced thanksgiving would be no gratitude at all, but a "wooden iron"), but also in the object-person to whom we are grateful and who gave us a freely given gift.[119] For, it would be senseless to thank anybody if we did not understand and believe that he acted freely as well as kindly towards us or to persons dear to us. We can neither thank a robot or marionette, nor a total egoist bereft of any spark of kindness and good-will. We have to refer the reader for the further development of this insight and argument for free will to other sources.[120]

Now, there is an important difference between our experience of our own free will and of that of other persons. For, while we experience our own free will with an immediate certainty and evidence from within, for example, when we experience our own guilt and repent of our sin, or experience our will to search the truth, we do not have the same *immediate* and, even less, the same intimate and *inner experience* of any other person's free will.

Someone might object to both sides of this remark and say: in the first place, we do not have less second-person certainty about another person's free will than about our own. In the second place, we do not have any evidence about our own free will at all, let alone a superior evidence. To claim such a superiority of first person free will experiences, or their evidence, would accordingly be an idol of self-knowledge.[121] For example, a scrupulous person might feel guilty when he is not guilty and has not even any good cause to feel such, while the hardened evildoer might feel innocent and unfree when he is as a matter of fact clearly free and responsible; hence we do not know our own free will best, but rather we know it quite badly and can be mistaken about it.

Now while this might be true of certain single instances, in which a scrupulous or schizophrenic patient may think he acted freely when he did act from compulsion, or a mass-murderer feels innocent, while he was coldly and freely carrying out his crime, it is not true about our intuition of our own free will and of human free will as such that it would be uncertain or fail to be more evident than our knowledge of other persons' free will. In fact, without an authentic experience of our own free will, the illusions of believing to have acted freely in a certain instance (where we have not done so) would be quite impossible; the experience of our true free will is the condition of the illusion of it in some instances. One might say quite generally: any error and aberration from the truth presupposes some true knowledge. Thus, also, any error about free will presupposes some experience of the true fact of human free will just as any other deception and error necessarily presupposes the knowledge of some truth without which and without whose experience and knowledge we could not be deceived.

The above remark about the different mode of experiencing existing free will in ourselves and in others must not seduce us into believing that we only know our own free will. For, while we know it with a unique inner evidence, nevertheless, when we forgive some wrong done to us by another person, or when we are grateful to another person, we not only necessarily presuppose, but also possess a certain degree of evidence of empathic knowledge, that he is a free agent.[122] The same is true when we exhort or praise, admonish, chide, condemn, or encourage another person. Moreover, there are certain sources of blindness of knowledge of our own responsibility and free will (for example, the pride that prevents us from admitting our guilt) that we do not fall into regarding the free will of others.

6. *There is also an argument on behalf of free will as a condition of efficient causality:* One can argue for free will also by taking one's starting point in the experience of causality and in a variety of insights into the essence of efficient causality. Doing so, one usually treats free will on a broader metaphysical level that does not restrict the consideration of free will to just human freedom. Arguments in favor of free will from causality invert some frequently advanced arguments against free will likewise based on certain (and, in my opinion, seriously mistaken) interpretations of the principles of causality or sufficient reason and of their implications.

Many philosophers object against free will by launching the claim that free will contradicts both the principle of causality, according to which any change and any contingent being presupposes an efficient cause through the power of which it becomes or is, and the much larger principle of sufficient reason that says that there must always exist, inside or outside of any changing or unchanging, necessary or contingent being, a reason that explains why something is rather than not being and why it is in a certain way rather than in any other way. Some draw from these two principles (that they recognize to be evident truths) the conclusion that free will cannot exist because it would contradict these two evident principles, and nothing that contradicts them can be true. Others claim that there is an antinomy here, because causality and the law of causality and of sufficient reason both presuppose and contradict free will. Given such an alleged contradiction, Kant and others conclude that no theoretical knowledge of free will is possible, but only a subjective moral postulate of free will valid for ethics, but not for theoretical philosophy. One can show, I would argue, that all such objections rest on a profound misapprehension of the principles of sufficient reason as well as of efficient causality. The latter says that every change and every contingent being presupposes an efficient cause through the action of which it comes about or is. This principle, when correctly stated, and not in the self-contradictory way of David Hume that every being presupposes a cause, or of Kant, who claims that every event follows upon another event according to a general law (rule), so little contradicts free will that any denial of free will and of an absolute beginning of causal chains in free acts leads to an absurd infinite regress of causes without any ultimate explanation of causality. For, as each cause would only possess and exert a causal force it would have received from a previous cause, and so on ad infinitum, there would be absolutely no explanation whatsoever of the beginning of efficient causality. An absurd infinite regress would result in a world in which causality would exist without free will, because there could be neither explanation nor beginning of a chain of efficient causes.[123] Moreover, efficient causality of material, biological, and other unfree causes not only necessarily presupposes at its beginning a causality through free will, but the acting person, the personal agent who acts freely, is also the archetype of efficient causality, wherefore also Aristotle speaks of a personal efficient cause, an *aitios,* more than of an impersonal cause, an *aitia,* when he introduces efficient causality in the context of his great discovery of the four causes.[124] As soon as one sees that free will itself is a primary kind of efficient cause and, likewise, is among the chief reasons why things are and, hence, an important part of the sufficient reasons for things, the construal of a contradiction between free will and causality or sufficient reason collapses.

Certainly, an interpretation of the principle of sufficient reason that interprets this principle, along some formulations of G. W. Leibniz, as requiring that each event and being must have a necessary reason contradicts free choice. Likewise, any view according to which the reason and cause of what is or happens in a being must lie outside that being, contradicts free will. For, if my decisions were caused by beings and events outside myself, for example, by my brain, by society, or by God, they could not be free.

This idea, however, neither follows from the true principle of causality nor from that of sufficient reason. On the contrary, this determinist thesis entirely ignores the primary reasons and causes in the universe: the personal ones.

Once one sees that every change and being must have a sufficient reason for being and for being in such and such a way and that this reason can either lie within a being or outside it, one will see that it is impossible that all reasons, namely, those of contingent, non-necessary things and of free acts, can be necessary reasons, or that all reasons can be reasons and causes extrinsic to a given being.

Among the non-necessary reasons, free decisions, far from contradicting this principle, are themselves an exceedingly important class or part of sufficient reasons, as they are also a primary sort of efficient cause. Moreover, while meaningful free acts require some motives, these motives must not have the character of necessitating reasons, but can be inviting reasons or obliging reasons or temptations and others that address themselves in very different ways to a person's free will without ever forcing it, precisely because the free decision or act of allowing these motives to motivate us is itself free. If these facts are contemplated, the whole opposition between causality and free will breaks entirely down, and the deep and necessary relations between both that we have discussed, and many others, emerge before our minds.

7. *A seventh argument or series of arguments for freedom can be gained from a refutation of the arguments that lie at the root of determinism and of Libet's denial of what he is calling positive free will.* Finally, we might argue in favor of free will by subjecting the various arguments against the existence of free will to a critical investigation, which we have already done in part, but shall enlarge upon at this point.

Having briefly recalled the objections against positive free will made by Libet, it is natural that we begin by a refutation of these and by showing first that his admission of the veto power of the will or "negative free will" logically presupposes that there is also "positive free will," for if there existed, as he suggests, a complete determination of all positive volitional acts and movements through preceding brain processes, this would precisely render impossible the act of interfering with such determined motions by a free veto. We see this most easily if we consider another experience that is clearly caused by preceding brain events such as horrific pains caused by a brain tumor. These pains are certainly caused from outside the conscious and free center of the person and hence are unfree, but it would contradict this unfree character of the headaches if by a veto we could make them disappear; since they are caused by the tumor in the brain and outside any control of our free will, we can precisely not make them disappear by a veto of our will.

In addition, there is a big lack of clarity regarding the meaning of "negative" and "positive" free will and the describing of the vetoing power of the mind in terms of some type of negative use of free will. Why should this veto be "negative freedom"? It seems clear first of all that Libet has in mind only one single kind of free vetoing act that interrupts, suppresses, or impedes physical movements, rather than looking at the wide spectrum of free acts, many of which are not connected with physical movements, but which we still might call "vetoing," "disavowing," "disallowing," "forbidding," or "rejecting"— for example, evil wishes, affections of envy, or evil thoughts and plans to commit a crime. Therefore, in order to deal with the question of whether there are free positive acts and what is the range of vetoing acts, Libet ought to have considered a far wider range of both of them in order to do justice to the problem he purports to solve.

Proceeding from his very narrow perspective of just considering free, or better, entirely arbitrary physical actions or physical movements, Libet calls negative freedom the act of not moving, and positive free will the carrying out of certain physical movements. In so doing, however, Libet to some extent remains a pure behaviorist who, notwithstanding his wish to take into consideration volitions, decisions, and other conscious acts, to a large degree identifies the observable positive physical behavior (of moving a limb), or at least the will that carries this movement out, with the positive free act, the freedom of which he denies, and therefore defines the free will of not moving as a mere negative and vetoing power of free will.

But if we consider the inner life of the free person, we see that the free act of a decision not to act is not comparable to the mere absence of moving in the physical world. Rather, we encounter equally positive and difficult free acts of omission as by commission of physical actions. For example, the decisions of the seven brothers described in the book of the *Maccabees* not to sacrifice to false gods, taking upon themselves the cruel death they suffered in consequence of this veto, is a far harder and more positive free act than a blind obedience to the evil king's command to break the divine law and to blaspheme or worship idols. Or why should the prophet Daniel's refusal to proclaim the king to be God, notwithstanding his being thrown into a lions' den, be a less positive free act than cowardly and foolishly to proclaim the Persian king as God? Only a pure behaviorist who understands nothing of free acts can hold that the idol worshippers performed a positive free act while the Maccabeans or Daniel did not perform a positive free act, speaking an inner yes that led them to a perfectly free "No"![125]

Here we observe again the logical contradiction in allowing for negative free will and disallowing positive one. For if Daniel and the Maccabeans had not been free to sacrifice to the gods, an action that according to Libet would have been forced on them by brain processes, how could they have been free to veto these acts? And if we can at any time modify voluntary movements, as our experience plentifully shows and Libet admits, why should this giving our movement another direction not be positive free will?

All of this makes Libet's claim that his experiments allow only the admission of a negative veto-role of free will both confused and unfounded.

Moreover, Libet seems to fail entirely to see the basic point of his experiments that has been so much better understood and explained by Popper and Eccles.[126] The central evidence of Libet's experiment precisely shows that, notwithstanding its being preceded in time by the readiness potential by milliseconds, the free decision to act at a certain time and the actual acting at this time, or also the preceding and accompanying free acts, make a tremendous new energy burst forth in the brain. And if the person suddenly decides not to act at a spontaneously chosen or a previously decreed given time, nothing happens and no physiologically wholly unexpected energies will emerge in the neurons, a fact Libet fully recognizes and on which he bases his thesis of the veto-power of free will!

But why then not admit that all empirical evidences only corroborate the opinion that the modular patterns of motion in the brain occur in form of a sudden appearance, quite independently of any preceding brain-state and precisely, only, and exactly then when the person on whom the experiment is performed wants to become active and does not veto his acts?[127]

The view that we have no free will at all is frequently defended by two other arguments: first, by claiming that the notion of free will is incoherent or even self-contradictory, and secondly, by claiming that free will would violate the "principle of causal closure" or "classical determinism" that are taken to be certainly true (without noticing that "classical determinism" ends up in a radical relativism because it denies not only free will, but also knowledge of the truth because of its failing to recognize the intentionality and transcendence of the act of knowledge and in virtue of its replacing the rational mental relation between subject and object by a notion of knowledge as causal effect of chemical, electrical, and biological efficient causes of cognition which are incompatible with knowledge).

According to this view, the material universe would have to be a causally closed whole in which there would be no room for any intrusion through outside forces or causes or any causes of non-physical nature, a view which not only an adequate philosophy of free will, but also of life in general, refutes, and which often is also based on a false understanding of the "law of the preservation of energy" that applies only to a closed system, while free will would precisely be a force and cause from outside the system of the material universe.[128] Neither for causal closure of the physical universe, nor for classical determinism is there the slightest evidence. On the contrary, they contradict themselves as well as the clear evidences for free will and rational knowledge, as we have seen in the discussion of the different arguments in favor of human free will. It depends entirely on the quality of these determinist positions and the arguments in favor of them, which we find faulty for many reasons partly alluded to in the previous argument, on the one hand, and on the quality of the positive arguments for the existence of free will which we found overwhelmingly and evidently true, whether we should accept that we have free will.

We have argued, that in at least a seven-fold way, we can indeed know that we are free and answer the question: "Do we possess free will?" with the unambiguous reply: "Yes, we do possess free will!" and what is the best: all of us, at least deep down in our most basic and elementary conscious experience, know this immensely important truth from childhood on, a truth that philosophy can only bring out from the dark into the light, just as a midwife helps the already existing child to reach the light of the day, thereby refuting the host of determinist negations of free will, including the partial one by Benjamin Libet.

ENDNOTES

1   Professor and Founding Rector of The International Academy of Philosophy in the Principality of Liechtenstein, 1986–, at the Pontificia Universidad Católica de Chile, 2004–2012, and in Granada, Spain, IAP-IFES, 2011–.

2   The first and second part of this book goes back to a Lecture held on October 20, 2010, as the opening address of the first Congress of the "Chilean Society of Christian Philosophy" entitled "Libertad y Filosofía Cristiana" (Oct. 20–22, 2010). A very similar text was translated into Italian and appeared as an Italian book (Milano: Morcellana, 2013). The third part of the present book, however, is considerably more extensive than in the Italian publication.

3   See: Emile Bréhier, "Y a-t-il une philosophie chrétienne?", *Revue de métaphysique et de morale* 38 (1931): 133–62:

> [O]ne can no more speak of a Christian philosophy than of a Christian mathematics or a Christian physics. ("Y-a-t'il," 162).

Bréhier also deplores the loss of autonomy of philosophy in this context, understanding "Christian philosophy" as an inauthentic philosophy that would be forced to submit to some extrinsic authority. He adds that if philosophy and reason are "forced in their exercise to submit to any external authority," this "calls into question the autonomy of reason that must have the lead and the initiative in philosophical thought." According to him the idea of "Christian Philosophy" leads to a "heteronomy of a reason completely incapable of directing itself" and "losing control over its own conclusions. ("Y-a-t'il," 150).

> See also the *Internet Encyclopaedia of Philosophy* [http://www.iep.utm.edu/chri1930/], "Christian Philosophy: The 1930s French Debates." This extremely interesting and well-researched article gives a detailed bibliography. For a detailed bibliography and overview of this French Debate see also "La notion de philosophie chrétienne," Session of 21 March

1931, *Bulletin de la Société française de Philosophie*, v. 31. This issue contains contributions and discussions engaging Étienne Gilson, Emile Bréhier, Jacques Maritain, Léon Brunschvicg, Edouard Le Roy, Raymond Lenoir, Maurice Blondel and Jacques Chevalier. See likewise, *La philosophie chétienne: Juvisy, 11 Septembre 1933*, which gives an account of the 2nd Day of Studies of the Société Thomiste (Paris: Cerf, 1933). This book demonstrates the intensity of the French debate, including contributions by M.D. Chenu, O. P., Aimé Forest, A.R. Motte, Étienne Gilson, Pierre Mandonnet, Antonin Sertillanges, Daniel Feuling, Masnovo, Cochet, Jacques Maritain, M.E. Baudin, Roland-Gosselin, O.P. , M.G. Rabeau, and Maurice Blondel. The article provides also a large bibliography on the question of a Christian philosophy, among which the following publications by Gabriel Marcel deserve special mention: "Position du mystère ontologique et ses approches concrètes," *Les Études Philosophiques* 7 (1933): 95–102 (with responses by Blondel and Bréhier), later translated in *Being and Having: An Existentialist Diary*, trans. Katherine Farrer (New York: Harper, 1965) 116–21.

4 The most adamant opponent of the idea of Christian philosophy in the 1930s was the Neo-scholastic Pierre Mandonnet, who wrote in the 1933 Société Thomiste meeting almost the same as Bréhier:

Certainly Christianity has transformed the world, but it has not transformed philosophy. . . . Certainly Christianity has been a considerable factor of progress in humanity, but not progress of a philosophical order. Progress in the philosophical order does not take place by Scripture but by reason. . . . Progress in philosophy therefore does not take place by the paths of religion. Even if there had been neither Revelation nor Incarnation, there would have been development of science and of thought. (*La philosophie chrétienne: Juvisy, 11 Septembre 1933*, 67–68)

Léon Noël expresses himself in a more differentiated way, apparently acknowledging at least one of our eleven valid senses of Christian philosophy when he writes in his paper "La notion de philosophie chrétienne," *ibid.*, 340):

Christian doctrines do not enter as such into the objective exposition of a philosophy, or then that philosophy would cease to be a philosophy. They cannot serve as such for the basis of a reasoning. But their presence in the mind of the believer can orient the research with a new meaning. ("La notion," 339–40)

Also Fernand Van Steenberghen holds a similar though even more moderate position:

There are *Christian philosophers*, because some Christians can give themselves over to philosophical research, and because their Christianity disposes them to give themselves over with perspicuity, with prudence, with serenity; it helps them with working out *a true philosophy*. To the degree that it is true, a philosophy is necessarily compatible with Christianity, open to Christianity, utilizable by Christianity and by theology; its content will be able to partially coincide with that of Revelation. But a philosophy will never be "Christian" in the formal and rigorous sense. One can, doubtless, speak of Christian philosophers in a purely material sense, to designate philosophies that have been worked out by Christian thinkers. But since the facts demonstrate the latent danger of this usage, it would be better to avoid using an expression that, far from illuminating anything, is a source of confusions and equivocations. ("La IIe journée d'études de la Société Thomiste et la notion de 'philosophie chrétienne,'" 554)

On them, Gilson writes (quoted from *Internet Encyclopaedia of Philosophy* [http://www.iep.utm.edu/chri1930/], "Christian Philosophy: The 1930s French Debates":

[A]ll of them agree with Saint Thomas that truth cannot contradict truth and that, consequently, what faith finds agrees substantially with what reason proves. They would even go further, for if faith agrees with reason, if not in its method, at least in its content, all factual disagreement between the two is an indication of an error in the philosophical order and a warning that one has to reexamine the problem. Still, all of the neo-Scholastic philosophers add that, insofar as philosophy, philosophy is the exclusive work of reason. (*Bul. Soc fr. Phil.*, 42)

5   See for example the following text on Gilson's position from *Internet Encyclopaedia of Philosophy* [http://www.iep.utm.edu/chri1930/], "Christian Philosophy: The 1930s French Debates":

> From rationalist perspectives, Patristic and Medieval thought, as well as those of their modern interpreters, would not legitimately deserve the title of philosophy. Gilson notes, however, holding that "everything that either directly or indirectly undergoes the influence of a religious faith ceases, ipso facto, to retain any philosophical value," really stems from and represents "a mere 'rationalist' postulate, directly opposed to reason." (*The Spirit of Medieval Philosophy*, 406).

6   The most famous of these took place in France in the 1930s. See *Internet Encyclopaedia of Philosophy* [http://www.iep.utm.edu/chri1930/], "Christian Philosophy: The 1930s French Debates":

> Between 1931 and 1935, important debates regarding the nature, possibility and history of Christian philosophy took place between major authors in French-speaking philosophical and theological circles. These authors include Etienne Gilson, Jacques Maritain, Maurice Blondel, Gabriel Marcel, Fernand Van Steenberghen and Antonin Sertillanges. The debates provided occasion for participants to clarify their positions on the relationships between philosophy, Christianity, theology and history, and they involved issues such as the relationship between faith and reason, the nature of reason, reason's grounding in the concrete human subject, the problem of the supernatural, and the nature and ends of philosophy itself. The debates led participants to self-consciously re-evaluate their own philosophical commitments and address the problem of philosophy's nature in a novel and rigorous manner.
>
> Although these debates originally took place between Roman Catholics and secular Rationalists, fundamental differences between different Roman Catholic positions rapidly became apparent and as-

sumed central importance. The debates also drew attention from Reformed Protestant thinkers. Eventually the debates sparked smaller discussions among scholars in English, German, Spanish, Portuguese and Italian-speaking circles, and these continue to the present day. This article provides a brief overview of the most important contributors, the central issues and the main positions of these debates.

7   On this matter, I also agree with Étienne Gilson. See *Internet Encyclopaedia of Philosophy* [http://www.iep.utm.edu/chri1930/], "Christian Philosophy: The 1930s French Debates":

> Gilson notes, however, holding that "everything that either directly or indirectly undergoes the influence of a religious faith ceases, ipso facto, to retain any philosophical value," really stems from and represents "a mere 'rationalist' postulate, directly opposed to reason." (*The Spirit of Medieval Philosophy*, 406)

8   By Gilson, Maritain, and other participants in the famous debates in France and later in many other countries.

9   For the same reason the decisive point of unity of a Society of Christian philosophy cannot be the common Creed alone even though one may reasonably hope that those who profess the apostolic or Nicene Creed have some common grounds also in philosophy. Nevertheless, it is clear from countless examples that adherence to the Creed in no way guarantees that the believer will espouse a philosophy compatible with his Christian faith and therefore we cannot accept the first definition of "Christian philosophy" as a meaningful and sufficient one but have to look for much more than a common Creed to understand its nature.

10   See Edmund Husserl, "Philosophie als strenge Wissenschaft," in Edmund Husserl, *Aufsätze und Vorträge* (1911–1921), ed. Thomas Nenon and Hans Rainer Sepp, *Husserliana* Bd. XXV (Dordrecht/Boston/Lancaster: M. Nijhoff, 1987), 3–62. See also Josef Seifert, "Phänomenologie und Philosophie als strenge Wissenschaft. Zur Grundlegung einer realistischen phänomenologischen Methode – in kritischem Dialog mit Edmund Husserls Ideen über die Philosophie als strenge Wissenschaft," in *Filosofie, Pravda, Nesmrtlenost. Tòi praúská pòednáóky/Philosophie, Wahrheit, Unsterblichkeit. Drei Prager Vorlesungen/ Philosophy, Truth, Immortality.*

Endnotes

Three Prague Lectures (tschechisch-deutsch), pòeklad, úvod a bibliografi Martin Cajthaml (Prague: Vydala Kòestanská akademie Òim, svacek, edice Studium, 1998), 14–50.

11 See Herman Dooyeweerd, "Introduction to transcendental criticism of philosophic thought," *Evangelical Quarterly* 19 (1947): 47–51; *A New Critique of Theoretical Thought*, 4 vols. (Philadelphia: Presbyterian and Reformed Pub. Co., 1953–58); *Roots of Western Culture: Pagan, Secular and Christian Options* (Toronto: Wedge, 1979).

12 William Young, "Herman Dooyeweerd," in *Creative Minds in Contemporary Theology*, ed. P. E. Hughes (Grand Rapids: Eerdmans, 1966), 270–306. http://www.freewebs.com/reformational/dooyeweerd.htm. Reproduced with the permission of the publisher. Please visit their website: www.eerdmans.com. William Young, "The Nature of Man in the Amsterdam Philosophy," *Westminster Theological Journal* 22 (1959): 1–12.

13 See Edmund Husserl, "Philosophie als strenge Wissenschaft."

14 This view reduces scientific Christian philosophy to a sphere of logic, language philosophy, and a kind of formalism that per se cannot answer any of the fundamental questions of philosophy. Consequently Christian philosophy would just explicate the Christian faith and be entirely dependent on it. Gilson mentions many other past cases of such a fideism ("theologism," as he calls it): *Internet Encyclopaedia of Philosophy* [http://www.iep.utm.edu/chri1930/], "Christian Philosophy: The 1930s French Debates":

> Gilson himself cited a number of past examples, including Tertullian, Peter Damian, the Franciscan spirituals, the *Imitation of Christ*'s anonymous author, Martin Luther and briefly discussed Karl Barth (*Christianity and Philosophy*, p. 44–48), remarking: "All the Barthian Calvinist asks of philosophy is that it recognize itself as damned and remain in that condition" (*Christianity and Philosophy*, p. 47).

See also the following poignant text of Karl Barth:

> There never actually has been a *philosophia christiana*, for if it was *philosophia* it was not *christiana*, and if it was *christiana* it was not *philosophia*. (*Church Dogmatics*, v. 1 , p. 6)

15 See H. T. Engelhardt, Jr., *The Foundation of Bioethics* (New York and Oxford: Oxford University Press, 1986), 2nd ed., Oxford University Press, 1996. See Lev Shestov, *Athens and Jerusalem*, 1937. In gen-

eral, Shestov disagrees with such a fideist position and defends an integration between Athens and Jerusalem. See also the following text of reformed philosophy:

> It is, however, an unwarranted prejudice to regard pre-theoretical common sense as more prone to error and uncertainty than theoretical science, and therefore to depreciate the cognitive claims of worldview as compared to those of philosophy. As a matter of fact, a good case can be made for the epistemological *priority* of worldview over philosophy. That is to say, philosophy (like all scientific knowing) is necessarily based on pre-scientific intuitions and assumptions that are given with the worldview of the philosopher concerned.
>
> . . . Van der Wal also explores the role of worldview in the philosophies of Spinoza and Leibniz, and comes to the general conclusion that pre-theoretical worldview and theoretical philosophy are like the two foci of an ellipse comprising all the giants of the philosophical tradition. . . . Rather than attempting the impossible task of doing philosophy in a worldview vacuum, philosophers should put their worldview cards on the table and enter the philosophical debate with none of those cards up their sleeve. Moreover, they should explicitly, self-consciously and unapologetically engage in philosophical systematics on the basis of their worldview. . . .
>
> For Christian philosophers, the obvious implication is that they must seek to orient their philosophizing to a Christian worldview. Or to put the case a bit more strongly and accurately, the Christian must seek to philosophize on the basis of the Christian worldview—that is, the *biblical* worldview. Presupposed in such a formulation *is* the conviction that there is one Christian worldview, and that it is taught in the Scriptures. . . .
>
> A Christian thinker whose worldview is dominated by a nature/grace dichotomy will still base his philosophizing on his worldview insofar as "natural reason" must allow for an area where sin and grace are decisive. But he will feel much more easily justified in following the current and

fashionable manifestations of that natural reason than a Calvinist who denies the existence of a purely "natural reason". . . .

The emphasis on the *religious* nature of philosophy also accounts for Bavinck's critique of Scottish common-sense philosophy, with its doctrine of an infallible intuition.

See also William Young, *Rationality in the Calvinian Tradition*, ed. H Hart, J van der Hoeven, and Nicholas Wolterstorff (Toronto: UPA, 1983), 113–31.

16 For example, I think of this one, which is, in my view, contradictory:

> I call Christian every philosophy which, although keeping the two orders formally distinct, nevertheless considers the Christian Revelation as an indispensable auxiliary to reason. . . . [T]he concept does not correspond to any simple essence susceptible of abstract definition; but corresponds much rather to a concrete historical reality as something calling for description. . . . [It] includes in its extension all those philosophical systems which were in fact what they were because a Christian religion existed and because they were ready to submit to its influence. (*The Spirit of Medieval Philosophy*, 37)

How can the two orders remain formally distinct and while faith is "an indispensable auxiliary to reason"?

17 See the counterposition in Josef Seifert, *Back to Things in Themselves. A Phenomenological Foundation for Classical Realism* (London: Routledge, 1987); the same author, *Discours des Méthodes. The Methods of Philosophy and Realist Phenomenology* (Frankfurt / Paris / Ebikon / Lancaster / New Brunswick: Ontos-Verlag, 2008). Dietrich von Hildebrand, *Was ist Philosophie?, aus dem Engl. übers. v. Fritz Wenisch*, in Hildebrand, *Gesammelte Werke*, Bd. I (Regensburg/Stuttgart: Habbel/Kohlhammer, 1976); the same author, *Sittlichkeit und ethische Werterkenntnis. Eine Untersuchung über ethische Strukturprobleme*, Habilitationsschrift (München: Bruckmann, 1918), completely reprinted in: *Jahrbuch für Philosophie und phänomenologische Forschung*, Band 5 (Halle: Niemeyer, 1922), 462–602. Sonderdruck der Habilitationsschrift, ebd. 1921. Reprint Vols. 3–6 (1916–1923) 1989. Bad Feilnbach 2: Schmidt Periodicals; 2nd ed. (unveränderter reprographischer Nachdruck, zusammen mit der Dissertation Die Idee der sittlichen Handlung), ed.

Dietrich-von-Hildebrand-Gesellschaft (Darmstadt: Wissenschaftliche Buchgesellschaft, 1969), 126–266; 3rd rev. ed. (Vallendar-Schönstatt: Patris Verlag, 1982): also in Spanish: *Moralidad y conocimiento ético de los valores*, trans. Juan Miguel Palacios (Madrid: Cristiandad, 2006).

18 Just think of the Salomonic philosophical sentences in the Old Testament or the books of Wisdom and Proverbs which are largely purely philosophical in nature.

19 Rom 2:13–15:

> 13 For it is not those who hear the law who are just in the sight of God; rather, those who observe the law will be justified.
>
> 14 For when the Gentiles who do not have the law by nature observe the prescriptions of the law, they are a law for themselves even though they do not have the law.
>
> 15 They show that the demands of the law are written in their hearts, while their conscience also bears witness and their conflicting thoughts accuse or even defend them

20 See my detailed critique of this position in chapter 5 (4–6) of *The Philosophical Diseases of Medicine and Their Cure. Philosophy and Ethics of Medicine, vol. 1: Foundations*, Philosophy and Medicine 82 (New York: Springer, 2004) – *Philosophical Diseases of Medicine and Their Cure. Philosophy and Ethics of Medicine, vol. 1: Foundations*, Philosophy and Medicine 82, Kluwer online e-book, 2005.

21 "Examine everything with discernment; keep what is good; keep your distance from every trace of evil" (1 Thess 5:21–22).

> King James Version: "Prove all things; hold fast that which is good." New American Standard Version 1995: "But examine everything carefully; hold fast to that which is good."

22 Motto of the International Academy of Philosophy in the Principality of Liechtensteinand in Granada (IAP-IFES), Spain.

23 Thomas would no doubt have continued to do so after having received new criticisms and encountered new insights in Hume, Kant, Hegel, Wittgenstein, etc. Also the encyclical of Pope John Paul II *Fides et ratio* completely rejects such a notion of Christian philosophy and *Aeterni Patris* of Leo XIII upon a closer reading— especially of the critique of those Thomists who reject all contributions of the Franciscan and other schools of

philosophy—already does not defend it.

24 See Immanuel Kant, *Die Religion innerhalb der Grenzen der bloßen
    Vernunft* (1793, zweite vermehrte Auflage, 1794). See also Im-
    manuel Kant, *Metaphysik der Sitten*, II, I, I, II. Hauptst., 2. Abschn.
    (Das, was Pflicht des Menschen gegen sich selbst ist, für Pflicht
    gegen andere zu halten.) § 18 (A 109), a. a. O., pp. 579 f.:

> *In Ansehung* dessen, was über unsere Erfahrungs-
> grenze hinaus liegt, aber doch seiner Möglichkeit
> nach in unseren Ideen angetroffen wird, z. B. der
> Idee von Gott, haben wir ebensowohl auch eine
> Pflicht, welche *Religionspflicht* genannt wird, die
> nämlich "der Erkenntnis aller unserer Pflichten *als*
> (instar) göttlicher Gebote." Aber dieses ist nicht das
> Bewußtsein einer Pflicht *gegen Gott.* Denn, *da diese
> Idee ganz aus unserer eigenen Vernunft hervorgeht, und
> von uns,* sei es in theoretischer Absicht, um sich die
> Zweckmäßigkeit im Weltganzen zu erklären, oder
> auch, um zur Triebfeder in unserem Verhalten zu
> dienen, von uns selbst *gemacht* wird, so haben wir
> hierbei nicht ein gegebenes Wesen vor uns, gegen
> welches uns Verpflichtung obläge: denn da müßte
> dessen Wirklichkeit allererst durch Erfahrung be-
> wiesen (geoffenbart) sein; sondern es ist die Pflicht
> des Menschen gegen sich selbst, diese unumgän-
> glich der Vernunft sich darbietende Idee auf das mo-
> ralische Gesetz in uns, wo es von der größten
> Fruchtbarkeit ist, anzuwenden.

25 Consider his belief that the essence of Christianity has to be un-
    derstood without faith by pure philosophical reason alone, which
    (probably only Hegel's own philosophy) according to him consti-
    tutes the highest form of the absolute spirit, in which God con-
    ducts a monologue with Himself and first comes to Himself. See
    Georg Friedrich Wilhelm Hegel, *Philosophie der Geschichte,* Jub. IX,
    12/26–27:

> Ich habe deshalb die Erwähnung, daß unser Satz,
> die Vernunft regiere die Welt und habe sie regiert,
> mit der Frage von der Möglichkeit der Erkenntnis
> Gottes zusammenhängt, nicht unterlassen wollen,
> um den Verdacht zu vermeiden, als ob die Philoso-
> phie sich scheue oder zu scheuen habe, an die reli-
> giösen Wahrheiten zu erinnern, und denselben aus
> dem Wege ginge, und zwar, weil sie gegen dieselben

sozusagen kein gutes Gewissen habe. Vielmehr ist es in neueren Zeiten so weit gekommen, daß die Philosophie sich des religiösen Inhalts gegen manche Art von Theologie anzunehmen hat. In der christlichen Religion hat Gott sich geoffenbart, das heißt, er hat dem Menschen zu erkennen gegeben, was er ist, so daß er nicht mehr ein Verschlossenes, Geheimes ist; es ist uns mit dieser Möglichkeit, Gott zu erkennen, die Pflicht dazu auferlegt. Gott will nicht engherzige Gemüter und leere Köpfe zu seinen Kindern, sondern solche, deren Geist von sich selbst arm, aber reich an Erkenntnis seiner ist und die in diese Erkenntnis Gottes allein allen Wert setzen. Die Entwicklung des denkenden Geistes, welche aus dieser Grundlage der Offenbarung des göttlichen Wesens ausgegangen ist, 12/27 muß dazu endlich gedeihen, das, was dem fühlenden und vorstellenden zunächst vorgelegt worden, auch mit dem Gedanken zu erfassen.

See also Georg Friedrich Wilhelm Hegel, *Phänomenologie des Geistes,* Jubiläumsausgabe Bd. 3. See also Winfried Weier, *Religion als Selbstfindung. Grundlegung einer Existenzanalytischen Religionsphilosophie* (Paderborn-München-Wien-Zürich: Ferdinand Schöningh, 1991).

26   See Michel Henri, *C'est moi la Vérité. Pour une philosophie du christianisme* (Paris: Éd. du Seuil, 1996); See also my chapter 5 "Ich bin die Wahrheit" in Josef Seifert, *Wahrheit und Person. Vom Wesen der Seinswahrheit, Erkenntniswahrheit und Urteilswahrheit,* De veritate – Über die Wahrheit Bd. I (Frankfurt / Paris / Ebikon / Lancaster / New Brunswick: Ontos-Verlag, 2009).

27   Similar criticical remarks could also be made about Karl Rahner's theology and others that are largely based on Hegel's or Heidegger's philosophies.

28   For example, in speaking of Christian mysteries as *absolute paradox* and praising Tertullian's *credo quia absurdum.* See Søren Kierkegaard, *Abschließende Unwissenschaftliche Nachschrift zu den philosophischen Brocken* (Ges. Werke 16. Abteilung) Teil I und II. (Düsseldorf/Köln: Diederichs, 1957/1958); the same author, *Das Buch Adler,* in S. Kierkegaard, *Einübung im Christentum und anderes,* ed. W. Rest (Köln und Olten: J. Hegner, 1951), 393–652. Also his praise of Lessing's famous word that appears to deny any knowledge of objective truth goes in the same direction. See G. E. Lessing,

Duplik, (1977); 213–15 . See also Herder, Briefe zur Beförderung der Humanität, pp. 874. (214–15) Digitale Bibliothek Sonderband: Meisterwerke deutscher Dichter und Denker, pp. 200–58 (vgl. Herder-HB Bd. 2, pp. 206–7):

"Nicht die Wahrheit, in deren Besitz irgendein
Mensch ist oder zu sein vermeinet, sondern die auf-
richtige Mühe, die er angewandt hat, hinter die Wahrheit zu kommen, macht den Wert des Menschen.
Denn nicht durch den Besitz, sondern durch die Nach-
forschung der Wahrheit erweitern sich seine Kräfte,
worin allein seine immer wachsende Vollkommen-
heit
bestehet. Der Besitz macht ruhig, träge, stolz -
Wenn Gott in seiner Rechten alle Wahrheit und in
seiner Linken den einzigen immer regen Trieb nach
Wahrheit, obschon mit dem Zusatz, mich immer und
ewig zu irren, verschlossen hielte und spräche zu
mir: ›Wähle!‹ Ich fiele ihm mit Demut in seine Linke
und sagte: ›Vater gib!‹ die reine Wahrheit ist ja doch
nur für dich allein!"

29   The Jewish philosopher Shestov also interprets Gilson's idea of Christian philosophy in that way, writing that for him
the revealed truth is founded on nothing, proves no-
thing, is justified before nothing, and—despite
this—is transformed in our mind into a justified, demonstrated, self-evident truth. Metaphysics wishes
to possess the revealed truth and it succeeds in
doing so. (*Athens and Jerusalem*, 271).

30   These reasons are more historical critical than philosophical.

31   See Hugo Staudinger, *Die historische Glaubwürdigkeit der Evangelien*, 7. Auflage, (Wuppertal und Zürich: R. Brockhaus, 1995).

32   Already the Jews at Jesus' time did not doubt the empty tomb but thought that the Apostles had bribed the guards and stolen Jesus' corpse. The Muslims believe that only a double of Jesus died and he himself was removed by God from his torturers. Superstitious people might believe in some superhuman body snatchers; scien-tists may believe in black holes into which Jesus' body fell, etc. Thus many admit the empty tomb but reject entirely the deeper spiritual and immensely mysterious reality of resurrection. There-

fore, even if a true philosophical task lies in this kind of philosophy of historicity and of apologetic demonstrations of the reality of the empty tomb, the described kind of "Christian philosophers" miss the point of Christianity if they believe that such reasonings can turn the awe-inspiring mysteries of incarnation or of resurrection and other mysteries of the Christian religion into transparent problems that can be solved or demonstrated by human philosophy instead of requiring an attitude of simple faith or a "Lord, I believe, help my unbelief."

33 See *Internet Encyclopaedia of Philosophy* [http://www.iep.utm. edu/chri1930/], "Christian Philosophy: The 1930s French Debates," which quotes the following forceful text of Gabriel Marcel:

> The contribution here is a certain datum—a revealed datum—whose signification, whose value is absolutely transcendent to any experience susceptible of being constituted on purely human bases. There is the paradox, the scandal, if you like. I would be disposed for my part, to think that there is Christian philosophy only there where this paradox, this scandal is not only admitted or even accepted, but *embraced* with a passionate and unrestricted gratitude. From the moment on when, to the contrary, philosophy seeks by some procedure to attenuate this scandal, to mask the paradox, to reabsorb the revealed datum in a dialectic of pure reason or mind, to this precise degree it ceases to be a Christian philosophy. ("A propos," 311–12)

34 See Richard Swinburne, The Resurrection of God Incarnate, (Oxford: Oxford University Press, 2003): See also Stephen T. Davis, *Risen Indeed: Making Sense of the Resurrection* (Grand Rapids, MI: Eerdmans, 1993) and Franz Klein, "Supernaturalism and Historical Study: An Account of the Resurrection of Jesus Christ from the Dead," *Quodlibet Journal 7* (2005); http://www.quodlibet.net/articles/klein-resurrection.shtml, who concludes:

> An argument is provided which proves that a supernatural explanation is the most probable explanation for the Resurrection based on the evidence provided in the canonical and extra-canonical books, and living tradition of the Church.

See likewise the interesting critique of Swinburne's views by pointing out that Christian faith requires a specific religious epistemology and source of certainty that cannot be reduced to purely rational probabilities: Paul K. Moser, "Critical Notice, Philosophy of Religion and Christian Resurrection," *International Journal of Philosophical Studies* 12 (2004): 61–69. See on a philosophy of resurrection also Nikolai Fyodorovich Fyodorov, *Philosophy of Physical Resurrection* (1906).

35 This group of thinkers either intends to demonstrate by purely philosophical reasons the truth of Christian Revelation, or content themselves with making its contents appear probable by means of philosophical arguments, such that the act of faith would assume the character of a rational decision regarding objective probabilities; other members of this group, for example Pannenberg, interpret faith with Pascal as a bet, or as a mere falsifiable hypothesis a la Popper.

36 See Blaise Pascal, *Pensées*, 418/233; Series II, 550b–551b. Pascal claims that we neither know the existence nor the essence of God and therefore have to decide and bet for one or the other side, between which we cannot remain neutral. And the chances being equal, we should bet on the side of God where we can only lose little and gain infinitely much: eternal beatitude. On the other side, we can gain only little and lose infinitely much. Hence pure logic of betting tells us that we should opt for faith. The most important part of the passage is the following:

> Oui, mais il faut parier. Cela n'est pas volontaire, vous êtes embarqués. Lequel prendrez-vous donc? Voyons; puisqu'il faut choisir voyons ce qui vous intéresse le moins. . . . Votre raison n'est pas plus blessée puisqu'il faut nécessairement choisir, en choisissant l'un que l'autre. Voilà un point vidé. Mais votre béatitude? Pesons le gain et la perte en prenant croix que Dieu est. Estimons ces deux cas: si vous gagnez vous gagnez tout, et si vous perdez vous ne perdez rien: gagez donc qu'il est sans hésiter. . . .
>
> Il faudrait jouer (puisque vous êtes dans la nécessité de jouer) et vous seriez imprudent lorsque vous êtes forcé à jouer de ne pas hasarder votre vie pour en gagner 3 à un jeu où il y a pareil hasard de perte et de gain. Mais il y a une éternité de vie de bonheur. Et cela étant quand il y aurait une infinité de hasards dont un seul serait pour vous, vous auriez encore raison de gager un pour avoir deux, et vous agirez de mauvais sens, en étant obligé à jouer,

de refuser de jouer une vie contre trois à un jeu où
d'une infinité de hasards il y en a un pour vous, s'il
y avait une infinité de vie infiniment heureuse à gagner: mais il y a ici une infinité de vie infiniment
heureuse à gagner, un hasard de gain contre un
nombre fini de hasards de perte et ce que vous jouez
est fini. Cela ôte tout parti partout où est l'infini et
où il n'y a pas infinité de hasards de perte contre
celui de gain. Il n'y a point à balancer, il faut tout
donner. Et ainsi quand on est forcé à jouer, il faut re-
noncer à la raison pour garder la vie plutôt que de
la hasarder pour le gain infini aussi prêt à arriver
que la perte du néant.

Car il ne sert de rien de dire qu'il est incertain
si on gagnera, et qu'il est certain qu'on hasarde, et
que l'infinie distance qui est entre la certitude de ce
qu'on expose et l'incertitude de ce qu'on gagnera
égale le bien fini qu'on expose certainement à l'infini
qui est incertain. Cela n'est pas ainsi. Tout joueur hasarde avec certitude pour gagner avec incertitude,
et néanmoins il hasarde certainement le fini pour gagner incertainement le fini, sans pécher contre la raison. Il n'y a pas infinité de distance entre cette
certitude de ce qu'on expose et l'incertitude du gain:
cela est faux. Il y a, à la vérité, infinité entre la certitude de gagner et la certitude de perdre, mais l'incertitude de gagner est proportionnée à la certitude
de ce qu'on hasarde selon la proportion des hasards
de gain et de perte. Et de là vient que s'il y a autant
de hasards d'un côté que de l'autre le parti est à
jouer égal contre égal. Et alors la certitude de ce
qu'on s'expose est égale à l'incertitude du gain, tant
s'en faut qu'elle en soit infiniment distante. Et ainsi
notre proposition est dans une force infinie, quand
il y a le fini à hasarder, à un jeu où il y a pareils hasards de gain que de perte, et l'infini à gagner.

Cela est démonstratif et si les hommes sont ca-
pables de quelque vérité celle-là l'est. . . .

Je vous dis que vous y gagnerez en cette vie, et
que à chaque pas que vous ferez dans ce chemin,
vous verrez tant de certitude de gain, et tant de

néant de ce que vous hasardez, que vous connaîtrez
à la fin que vous avez parié pour une chose certaine,
infinie, pour laquelle vous n'avez rien donné.

37   Such a bet is something entirely different than faith, even though
one might justifiedly doubt whether such an interpretation of the
Pascalian "bet" does justice to the deepest sense of his comparing
a life based on religious faith with the only rational bet man ought
to take. See the preceding note.

38   A *fremdpersonaler Akt.* See on this notion Adolf Reinach, "Die aprio-
rischen Grundlagen des bürgerlichen Rechtes," in Adolf Reinach,
Sämtliche Werke. Texkritische Ausgabe in zwei Bänden, Bd. I: *Die
Werke,* Teil I: Kritische Neuausgabe (1905–1914), Teil II: Nachge-
lassene Texte (1906–1917); ed. Karl Schuhmann and Barry Smith
(München und Wien: Philosophia Verlag, 1989), 141–278.

39   1 Cor 1:18–25, especially:

20 Where is the wise man? Where is the scholar?
Where is the philosopher of this age? Has not God
made foolish the wisdom of the world? 21 For since
in the wisdom of God the world through its wisdom
did not know him, God was pleased through the
foolishness of what was preached to save those who
believe. 22 Jews demand miraculous signs and
Greeks look for wisdom, 23 but we preach Christ
crucified: a stumbling block to Jews and foolishness
to Gentiles, 24 but to those whom God has called,
both Jews and Greeks, Christ the power of God and
the wisdom of God. 25 For the foolishness of God is
wiser than man's wisdom, and the weakness of God
is stronger than man's strength.

See on this also Josef Seifert, *San Pablo y Santo Tomás sobre Fides et
ratio. ¿Fue San Pablo el crítico más severo o, con Santo Tomás, el defensor
más grande de la filosofía? Saint Paul and Saint Thomas. Was Saint Paul
the most severe Critic, or, with Saint Thomas the greatest defender of
Philosophy* (Madrid: Publicaciones de la Facultad de Teología "San
Dammaso," 2009). Christian philosophers of this genre frequently
also question the character of Christianity as resting on faith and
requiring a gift of grace and explain it purely naturalistically or as
being a mere object of philosophical thoughts.

40   In much of ancient and medieval, and also Muslim and Jewish,
and thus also in *not specifically Christian* philosophy, is much of
"Christian philosophy" in this first sense. A Christian philosopher

might interpret these as ultimately coming from God. As Justin the martyr, a philosopher, put it: "Any truth found anywhere is of the Holy Spirit and therefore is ours." Saint Justin the Martyr: "all that is beautiful which has been expressed by anyone, belongs to us Christians" (II Apologia 13,4).

41   Thus many of those elements that Clement of Alexandria calls "spermata tou logou" and that also Tertullian attributes to pre-Christian pagan philosophy in his expression of the "anima naturaliter Christiana" belong to such a true philosophy compatible with the faith. It is such fragments of true and therefore "Christian philosophy" in this sense that are referred to in the exhortation of Saint Paul to Christians: "examine everything; keep what is good."

See Carlo Tibiletti, "Tertulliano e la dottrina dell'Anima naturaliter christiana," in *Atti dell'Accademia delle Scienze di Torino* (1953/1954), 84–117 (Details A. Nicolotti).

42   See my discussion of different senses of "coherence" in my critique of the coherence theory of truth in chapter 2 of Josef Seifert, *Der Streit um die Wahrheit. Wahrheit und Wahrheitstheorien. De Veritate – Über die Wahrheit*, Bd. II / *The Fight about Truth. Truth and Truth Theories* (Frankfurt / Paris / New Brunswick: Ontos, 2009).

43   This corpus veritatis, but also each authentic part of it, is eo ipso, qua being true, not only compatible both with the knowledge already gained and expressed in various philosophical works and schools, and with the one still to be discovered, but also with Revelation. We find, however, at least some elements of such a "Christian" philosophy, i.e., a philosophy deeply akin to and compatible with Christian faith, in virtually any philosophical school none of which consists of nothing but errors or fails to contain even some true insights into issues relevant to Christian faith.

44   Most of the sentences of Thomas Aquinas and of Rosmini that were condemned by Church authorities, as well as the Thomist teaching on late ensoulment of the embryo, a mistaken idea of huge negative consequences in today's bioethical discussions that was condemned by the Church in *Evangelium Vitae*, fall into this group.

45   Of which Balduin Schwarz speaks, attributing its having reached, at least as a largely achieved goal, to Thomas Aquinas:

There was a great threat for the spiritual world to break apart, the old appeared worthy of respect but impotent; the new appeared fascinating but disruptive. It is the incomparable merit of Saint Thomas to have approached the situation of his time with no other question than with that of truth. Through the mere defense of a tradition, the mere hint at its greatness, at the authorities which stand behind it, one cannot banish such an elementary event as the becoming apparent of new aspects of reality. Thomas possessed the intellectual „nerves" – if we are allowed to use this term – to distance himself from the safe grounds of Augustinianism. Instead of seeking, in order to save as much as possible, a compromise with the New (i.e., with the Arab and Latin averroistic Aristotelianism), he loved simply the truth and was convinced of its unity, and thus began the gigantic process of the scrutiny of his opponent, the anti-Christian Aristotelianism, and of the clarification, transformation, and new rethinking of Aristotle. Simultaneously he also began a keen examination of the augustinian teaching, in order to unite everything in the unity of the single great *Corpus veritatis*. Reneging not the slightest part of truth, never thinking in terms of schools or cliques, ready to learn from everybody, never forgetting the whole over the part, and seeing with incomparable intellectual strength everything in its connection, careful and generous, flexible for every nuance, but keeping his eye unwaveringly directed at the *Totum*, calm in the progression of thought, never in doubt and caught in details, this became the genius of the *Summa*, of a high point of human existence. The positive response to a crisis and its mastering probably never was accomplished in such great purity, so wholly convincingly, so universally and forcefully. Without the intellectual deed of Saint Thomas the occident would have been ripped apart and deprived of its inner unity two centuries earlier, because it would not have kept present to itself the unity of being. But now again a whole and inclusive image of things was presented, in which everything known heretofore was placed at its right place, possessed its proper weight, as it befitteth the thing; and thereby it became clear in its unity and in its difference from everything else.

And at the same time the unity of the living

spiritual stream was preserved throughout the centuries.... The golden chain of history linked the present with the past.

Thomas may be regarded as the classical type of the genuine liberator from a spiritual crisis. He represents in the history of the mind the good and truly living forces, which a man awakens in himself when he integrates in his life something which he encounters at first as something threatening, or fascinating, but at any rate as something revolutionary and disruptive. Condition [of such an integration] is that he leads the line of life upward, uniting in his vibrant vigilant strength force, audacity and reverence, does not reject anything valuable, but lets it become stronger, does not anxiously repress anything new, but confronts it, resists its assault, banishes its power to fascinate, transforming it into the force of truth and making it part of himself and of his world. One ought to look onto Thomas, to the silent audacity of his spiritual deed, and not on any one of the overbearing revolutionaries without sense of responsibility in the sphere of the intellect, in order to get a sense of the significant truth of the famous saying of Nietzsche: "How much truth does a mind bear, how much truth does he dare? This became for me more and more the real criterion of value. Error is not blindness, error is cowardice... Every achievement, every step forward in knowledge follows from the courage, from the harshness against himself, from the clarity vis-à-vis oneself."

My own translation from the German: Balduin Schwarz, *Ewige Philosophie. Gesetz und Freiheit in der Geistesgeschichte* (Leipzig: Verlag J. Hegner, 1937; 2. Aufl. Siegburg: Schmitt, 2000), pp. 120–123.

46 This is true even though, however, the first important positive sense of Christian philosophy—a philosophy that would be perfectly compatible with Christian faith—remains, at least in part, more an ideal than a completed reality and, because of the loftiness of this goal, cannot be identified with any one existing school of philosophy as if it were *the* truth and *the* Christian philosophy. Although even highpoints of historical forms of Christian philosophy, such as Augustinian or Thomist philosophy, Anselmianism and Skotism, phenomenological realism and personalism, remain

imperfect historical embodiments of *a pure and heavenly Christian philosophy* perfectly *compatible with faith,* we encounter in some philosophies so many elements of such a true philosophy compatible with Christian faith that we can speak of authentic historical embodiments of such a Christian philosophy compatible with faith.

47 This sense of Christian philosophy was expounded by Alvin Plantinga in the IAP (The International Academy of Philosophy) Conference of 1983 in Dallas, Texas, on the reality of God and human dignity.

48 This even extends to the topic of bodily resurrection and anthropological reasons to expect it or hope for it, a theme that certainly is present in the Prophet Daniel and in some Muslim sources. In our secular, pluralistic and often atheistic society there is a certain courage necessary to pick up such topics, especially from a systematic viewpoint, and at the present moment in the history of philosophy Christian philosophers may have paid more attention to them than others. Moreover, some of these topics—for example, possible and impossible forms of "divine incarnation"—concern only Christian philosophers.

49 Gabriel Marcel may have this in mind when he speaks of the inner fruitful relation of any thought worth mentioning with all other important thoughts. See *Internet Encyclopaedia of Philosophy* [http://www.iep.utm.edu/chri1930/], "Christian Philosophy: The 1930s French Debates":
> If it was admitted that Christianity has had no positive influence on philosophical development, this would entail saying that it has never actually been able to be thought—for there is no thought worthy of that name that does not contribute to transforming all the other thoughts. . . . To say that Christianity has never been thought is to let it be understood that it is not thinkable. ("A propos de *L'esprit de la Philosophie médiévale* par M. E. Gilson," 309)

50 It also shows us realities which shed light on the world but of which human reason per se has no inkling such as the mystery of the Trinity.

51 See on this Étienne Gilson, *Die Philosophie des hl. Bonaventura,* 2nd ed. (Köln: Hegener, 1960).

52 At first sight the image of the cave (Plato, *Politeia,* 7.514 a ff.) seems to say the opposite because the philosopher who has seen only images and artifacts of things in the cave and is then taken outside the

cave and sees the real world in the sunlight, upon returning into the cave is blinded and unable to identify the shadows so that he becomes the object of the scorn of his fellow-prisoners and cavemen. However, in other passages of the Platonic text we find strong analogies to Bonaventure's image except that these are not applied to faith.

53 This position is basically also present in Étienne Gilson, though not without being vitiated at times by some fideistic elements. In general, and quite especially in his *L'Esprit de la philosophie médiévale* (Paris: Librairie philosophique J. Vrin, 1932) and in his *Die Philosophie des hl. Bonaventura*, 2nd ed. (Köln: Hegener, 1960), Gilson seems to defend both philosophy as a rational natural science that does not presuppose faith but is inspired by faith to perceive truth better. However, he expresses himself frequently as if Christian philosophy just took its starting point in faith or also as a philosopher who comes to understand with pure reason the mysteries of faith he first believes, another one of the five concepts of Christian philosophy we found fundamentally flawed. For example, he expresses both or either one of them, somewhat ambiguously, in the following passage in his *L'Esprit de la philosophie medieval:*

> This effort of truth believed to transform itself into truth known, is truly the life of Christian wisdom, and the body of rational truths resulting from the effort is Christian philosophy itself. Thus the content of Christian philosophy is that body of rational truths discovered, explored or simply safeguarded, thanks to the help reason receives from Revelation. (p. 35)

> Unless the expression be emptied of all positive content it must be frankly admitted that nothing less than an intrinsic relation between Revelation and reason will suffice to give it meaning. (Ibid.)

See also Étienne Gilson: *Being and Some Philosophers*, 2nd ed. (Toronto: University of Toronto Press, 1952); *The Elements of Christian Philosophy* (Garden City, NY: Doubleday, 1960); *Der heilige Augustin. Eine Einführung in seine Lehre*, trans. P.Philotheus Böhner and P.Timotheus Sigge (Leipzig: Hellerau, 1930); *Thomism* (5th ed.). See also my critique of some elements of Gilson's view in Josef Seifert, "Esse, Essence, and Infinity: a Dialogue with Existentialist Thomism," *The New Scholasticism* 58 (1984): 84–98; and my "Essence and Existence. A New Foundation of Classical Metaphysics on the Basis of 'Phenomenological Realism,' and a Critical Investigation of 'Existentialist Thomism'," *Aletheia* 1 (1977): 17–

157; 371–459.

   A far more complete version of my philosophy of essence and existence and critique of certain positions of existentialist Thomism is contained in my *Sein und Wesen*. Philosophy and Realist Phenomenology. Studies of the International Academy of Philosophy in the Principality Liechtenstein, Vol. 3 (Heidelberg: Universitätsverlag C. Winter, 1996).

54 Jacques Maritain, *Essay*, 23.

55 Maritain emphasized this point as well as the influence Christian virtues can exert on philosophy. See *Internet Encyclopaedia of Philosophy* [http://www.iep.utm.edu/chri1930/], "Christian Philosophy: The 1930s French Debates":

> Maritain distinguishes two main ways in which Christianity aids the activity of philosophy in concrete states: objective contributions and subjective reinforcements. Christianity makes objective contributions by supplying philosophy with data and ideas. Some of these "belong within the field of philosophy, but . . . philosophers failed to recognize [them] explicitly" (*Essay*, p. 18), e.g. the ideas of creation or of sin. Others are "objective data which philosophy knew well but which it approached with much hesitancy and which . . . was corroborated by Revelation" (*Essay*, p. 21).

56 In a number of texts, Gilson seems to defend this position, and perhaps even more clearly Jacques Maritain who distinguishes the essence of philosophy from its historical state and writes in his *An Essay on Christian Philosophy*, p. 7–11, 55–61, and *Science and Wisdom*, p. 82–86 (see *Internet Encyclopaedia of Philosophy* [http://www.iep.utm.edu/chri1930/], "Christian Philosophy: The 1930s French Debates"), though I find his manner of expressing himself still unclear and misleading, because such a divorce between essence and state of philosophy seems untenable and the claim that a pure philosophy such as that of Aristotle is a "monster" wholly unfounded and smacking of fideism:

> [W]e must distinguish between the *nature* of philosophy, or what it is in itself, and the state in which it exists in real fact, historically, in the human subject, and which pertains to its concrete conditions of existence and exercise. (*Essay*, p. 11–12)
>   In its nature or essence, philosophy is "intrinsically a natural and rational form of knowledge"

(*Essay*, p. 14), entirely independent from faith. As a form of knowledge, philosophy is specified by its object(s): "within the realm of the real, created and uncreated . . . a whole class of objects which are of their nature attainable through the natural faculties of the human mind" (*Essay*, p. 14). In its nature, however, philosophy is a pure abstract essence. It is all too easy a matter to endow such an abstraction with reality, to clothe it as such with a concrete existence. An ideological monster results; such, in my opinion, occurred in the case both of the rationalists and the neo-Thomists whom Mr. Gilson has called to task (*Essay*, p. 14).

Clearer is the following text that seems to come close to the valid sense of Christian philosophy we presently discuss:

> Christian philosophy is not a determinate body of truths, although, in my opinion, the doctrine of St. Thomas exemplifies its amplest and purest form. Christian philosophy is philosophy itself in so far as it is situated in those utterly distinctive conditions of existence and exercise into which Christianity has ushered the thinking subject, and as a result of which philosophy perceives certain objects and validly demonstrates certain propositions, which in any other circumstances would to a greater or lesser extent elude it. (*Essay*, p. 30)

57 See for example Plato's, *The Apology of Socrates*, the VIIth letter, the sixth book of his *Politeia*, his *Gorgias*, *Phaedo*, or his *Sophist*. See also Paola Premoli De Marchi, *Chi è il filosofo? Platone e la questione del dialogo mancante*, con Prefazione di Giovanni Reale (Milano: Franco Angeli, 2008).

58 This may be one central, if not *the* central, point in Mátyás Szalay's deep paper *philosophari in Maria*.

59 And objectively, as the believer will acknowledge, presuppose a spiritual Christian life and the aid of grace without which these virtues cannot be gained.

60 The error of denying free will, as I will try to show, negates the whole of Christian Revelation in such a radical way that not one single dogma of the faith can remain intact without free will being presupposed.

61 A non-believing philosopher, or one who perhaps struggles with the faith, might very well have a profound philosophical under-

standing of truths about the nature and existence of freedom and about the fact that Christian faith presupposes and does not, as some interpreted it, contradict human free will. He may perfectly well understand, far better than many Christians, that divine and human free will is necessarily presupposed by many contents of faith, and in which way and for which reasons this is the case.

62 The role Scheler's analyses of the Saint and humility, etc., played for several phenomenologists such as Saint Edith Stein is well known. For me it played the role of a kind of second conversion.

63 John 3:16: "For God so loved the world, that He gave His only begotten Son, that whoever believes in Him should not perish, but have eternal life."

64 According to my knowledge, Bergson converted on his death bed to the Catholic Church but had not taken this step when he defended in his *Les deux sources de la morale et de la religion* (Paris: F. Altan, 1932) the view that no morality is higher than that of the Christian mystics and that it is of a quality far superior to any non-Christian form of virtue.

65 In this sense, for example, Thomas Aquinas, Augustine, Bonaventure and many other Christian philosophers, Dietrich von Hildebrand, Max Scheler, Søren Kierkegaard, but also Henri Bergson, a non-Christian, were Christian philosophers.

66 For example, Augustine, Anselm of Canterbury (Aosta), John Henry Cardinal Newman, and many other spiritual writers like Thomas a Kempis, Francis de Sales, or Michel d'Elbée (see the latter's magnificent book, *Croire à l'amour*).

67 Max Scheler was probably the first great phenomenologist who presented extraordinary analyses of this in his works, *Zur Rehabiltierung der Tugend*, in M. Scheler, *Vom Umsturz der Werte* (Bern-München: Francke-Verlag, 1955); as well as in his *Das Ressentiment im Aufbau der Moralen*, in M. Scheler, *Vom Umsturz der Werte* (Bern-München: Francke-Verlag, 1955), in his *Der Formalismus in der Ethik und die materiale Wertethik: Neuer Versuch der Grundlegung eines ethischen Personalismus*, ed. Maria Scheler, 5th ed., Gesammelte Werke, Bd. 2 (Bern: A. Francke, 1966), as well in his "Ordo amoris," in Max Scheler, *Schriften aus dem Nachlaß*, Band I, ed. Manfred S. Frings, with an appendix by Maria Scheler, 3rd ed. (Bern: Bonn, Bouvier-Verlag, 1986; 1.–2. ed. in Francke Verlag), Gesammelte Werke, Bd. 10, 345–76. A more profound and reliable and theoretically much better founded Christian philosophy in the sense of a philosophy *of Christian data* was developed by Dietrich von Hildebrand. See Dietrich von Hildebrand, *Ethics*, 2nd

ed. (Chicago: Franciscan Herald Press, 1978), especially the last chapter and the *Prolegomena*; originally published under the title *Christian Ethics* (New York: David McKay, 1953 / Toronto: Musson, 1954 / London: Thames & Hudson, 1954 / *Ética cristiana*, trans. S. Gómez Nogales, S. J. (Barcelona: Editorial Herder, 1962); the same book later had the more fitting title *Ethik* under which it also was published in the original second English edition and translated into other languages; see Dietrich von Hildebrand, *Ethik*, in Dietrich von Hildebrand, *Gesammelte Werke*, Band II (Stuttgart: Kohlhammer, 1973); *Etica*, trans. Juan José García Norro (Madrid: Ediciones Encuentro, 1983). The concrete analysis of the essences of specifically Christian virtues, in contrast to their many pseudo / forms that can easily be seen through philosophical essential analysis has been presented masterfully by Dietrich von Hildebrand in his *Transformation in Christ. On the Christian Attitude of Mind*, last edition with a new sub-title: *Transformation in Christ. Our Path to Holiness*. Reprint of 1948 (New Hampshire: Sophia Institute Press. 1989). See also Dietrich von Hildebrand, *The Heart. An Analysis of Human and Divine Affectivity*, ed. by John Henry Crosby; Preface by John Haldane; Introduction by John F. Crosby; Edmund Husserl on Dietrich von Hildebrand, (South Bend, Indiana: St. Augustine's Press, 2006), and Dietrich von Hildebrand: *The Nature of Love*, trans. John F. Crosby with John Henry Crosby (South Bend: St. Augustine's Press, 2009); *Jaws of Death: Gate of Heaven*. Foreword by Alice von Hildebrand. Appendices: A. Wagner's relation to Schopenhauer; B. Hope, expectation, wishing, & desire; C. The formal objects of hope; D. Love of Jesus and love of neighbor. (Manchester, New Hampshire: Sophia Institute Press, 1991).

68 This was what Edith Stein experienced upon reading the *Autobiography* of Saint Teresa of Avila for a whole night.

69 See Dietrich von Hildebrand, *The Sacred Heart. An analysis of human and divine affectivity* (Baltimore / Dublin: Helicon Press, 1965), 2nd ed.: *The Heart* (Chicago: Franciscan Herald Press, 1977). *El corazón. Un análisis de la afectividad humana y divina* (Madrid: Ed. Palabra, 1997).

70 See on this Joseph Ratzinger / Benedict XVI, *El Dios de la fe y el Dios de los filósofos*, (Barcelona: Taurus, 1962); the same author, "Cristianismo: La victoria de la inteligencia sobre el mundo de las religiones," *Trenta Dias en la Iglesia y en el Mundo* 2000 (I), 49–60.

71 Clement of Alexandria held the view that Christianity is the true philosophy, and the perfect Christian the true "Gnostic according

to the canon of the Church." He even sees in his *Stromata* I, 5, philosophy as more than compatible with faith but as a handmaid of faith and an educator towards Christ, paidagwgovÀ eijÀ cristovn:

> Perchance, too, philosophy was given to the Greeks directly and primarily, till the Lord should call the Greeks. For this was a schoolmaster to bring "the Hellenic mind," as the law, the Hebrews, "to Christ." Philosophy, therefore, was a preparation, paving the way for him who is perfected in Christ.

72 This is a historical fact Balduin Schwarz made the key to understanding the difference between the ancient and medieval periods of the history of philosophy. See Balduin Schwarz, *Über das innere Prinzip der Periodisierung der Philosophiegeschichte*, Salzburger Universitätsreden, No. 7 (Salzburg-Münster: A. Pustet, 1966). See also his *Wahrheit, Irrtum und Verirrungen. Die sechs großen Krisen und sieben Ausfahrten der abendländischen Philosophie*, ed. Paula Premoli and Josef Seifert (Heidelberg: C. Winter, 1996).

73 More than any Greek philosopher does the God of the Old Testament and Christ criticize the false and superstitious elements of the religion of the Pharisees and religious errors of the Sadducees.

74 It applies to areas open to intuition into, and demonstrations of, essentially necessary data only to the extent to which we can rightfully be self-critical and take into account that sometimes, in the face of aporias, we confuse a mere incomprehensibility for human reason with an absolute impossibility, or superextend objective essential necessities to phenomena to which they do not apply, as, for example, when a philosopher holds that the idea of "original sin" contradicts the essentially necessary truth that a morally evil act and sin can only proceed from a person's abuse of his free will; in this case we do not understand that "original sin" is "sin" in a very different and mysterious sense. Or when we claim that divine omniscience or omnipotence excludes human freedom, we confuse incomprehensible apories and mysteries for our finite mind with absolute essential impossibilities. See on these natural mysteries also the magnificent text of René Descartes, *Principia philosophiae*, in *Oeuvres de Descartes*, ed. Charles Adam and Paul Tannery (Paris: Librairie Philosophique J. Vrin, 1982), Vol. VIII-1, Part I, 41–42. Descartes writes:

> In considering this more attentively, it occurs to me in the first place that I should not be astonished if my intelligence is not capable of comprehending

why God acts as He does; and that there is thus no reason to doubt of His existence from the fact that I may perhaps find many other things besides this as to which I am able to understand neither for what reason nor how God has produced them. For, in the first place, knowing that my nature is extremely feeble and limited, and that the nature of God is on the contrary immense, incomprehensible, and infinite, I have no further difficulty in recognising that there is an infinitude of matters in His power, the causes of which transcend my knowledge; . . . for it does not appear to me that I can without temerity seek to investigate the [inscrutable: The passages are not in the French but only in the original Latin version.] ends of God. (René Descartes, *Meditations*, 9th printing, in two volumes, trans. E. S. Haldane and G. R.T. Ross (Cambridge/London/New York: Cambridge University Press, 1973), 1:173)

On the notion of natural mystery and aporia see also the magnificent text by John Henry Cardinal Newman, *Parochial and Plain Sermons*, Sermon xix, "The mysteriousness of our present being":

1. First, we are made up of soul and body. Now, if we did not know this, so that we cannot deny it, what notion could our minds ever form of such a mixture of natures, and how should we ever succeed in making those who go only by abstract reason take in what we meant? The body is made of matter; this we see; it has a certain extension, make, form, and solidity: by the soul we mean that invisible principle which thinks. We are conscious we are alive, and are rational; each man has his own thoughts, feelings, and desires; each man is one to himself, and he knows himself to be one and indivisible, – one in such sense, that while he exists, it were an absurdity to suppose he can be any other than himself; one in a sense in which no material body which consists of parts can be one. He is sure that he is distinct from the body, though joined to it, because he is one, and the body is not one, but a collection of many things. He feels moreover that he is distinct from it, because he uses it; for what a man can use, to that he is superior. No one can by any possibility mistake his

body for himself. It is his; it is not he. This principle, then, which thinks and acts in the body, and which each person feels to be himself, we call the soul. We do not know what it is; it cannot be reached by any of the senses; we cannot see it or touch it. It has nothing in common with extension or form; to ask what shape the soul is, would be as absurd as to ask what is the shape of a thought, or a wish, or a regret, or a hope. And hence we call the soul spiritual and immaterial, and say that it has no parts, and is of no size at all. All this seems undeniable. Yet observe, if all this be true, what is meant by saying that it is in the body, any more than saying that a thought or a hope is in a stone or a tree? How is it joined to the body? what keeps it one with the body? what keeps it in the body? what prevents it any moment from separating from the body? when two things which we see are united, they are united by some connexion which we can understand. A chain or cable keeps a ship in its place; we lay the foundation of a building in the earth, and the building endures. But what is it which unites soul and body? how do they touch? how do they keep together? how is it we do not wander to the stars or the depths of the sea, or to and fro as chance may carry us, while our body remains where it was on earth? So far from its being wonderful that the body one day dies, how is it that it is made to live and move at all? how is it that it keeps from dying a single hour? Certainly it is as incomprehensible as any thing can be, how soul and body can make up one man; and, unless we had the instance before our eyes, we should seem in saying so to be using words without meaning. For instance, would it not be extravagant, and idle to speak of time as deep or high, or of space as quick or slow? Not less idle, surely, it perhaps seems to some races of spirits to say that thought and mind have a body, which in the case of man they have, according to God's marvellous will. It is certain, then, that experience outstrips reason in its capacity of knowledge; why then should reason circumscribe faith, when it cannot compass sight?

2. Again: the soul is not only one, and without parts, but moreover, as if by a great contradiction even in terms, it is in every part of the body. It is no where, yet every where. It may be said, indeed, that it is especially in the brain; but, granting this for argument's sake, yet it is quite certain, since every part of his body belongs to him, that a man's self is in every part of his body. No part of a man's body is like a mere instrument, as a knife, or a crutch might be, which he takes up and may lay down. Every part of it is part of himself, it is connected into one by his soul, which is one. Supposing we take stones and raise a house. The building is not really one; it is composed of a number of separate parts, which viewed as collected together, we call one, but which are not one except in our notion of them. But the hands and feet, the head and trunk, form one body under the presence of the soul within them. Unless the soul were in every part, they would not form one body; so that the soul is in every part, uniting it with every other, though it consists of no parts at all. I do not of course mean that there is any real contradiction in these opposite truths; indeed, we know there is not, and cannot be, because they are true, because human nature is a fact before us. But the state of the case is a contradiction when put into words; we cannot so express it as not to involve an apparent contradiction; and then, if we discriminate our terms, and make distinctions, and balance phrases, and so on, we shall seem to be technical, artificial and speculative, and to use words without meaning.

Now, this is precisely our difficulty, as regards the doctrine of the Ever-blessed Trinity. We have never been in heaven; God, as He is in Himself, is hid from us. We are informed concerning Him by those who were inspired by Him for the purpose, nay by One who "knoweth the Father," His Co-eternal Son Himself, when He came on earth. And, in the message which they brought to us from above, are declarations concerning His nature, which seem to run counter the one to the other. He is revealed to us as One God, the Father, One indivisible Spirit; yet there is said to exist in Him from everlasting His Only-begotten Son, the same as He is, and yet distinct, and from and in Them both, from everlasting and indivisibly, exists the Co-equal Spirit. All this, put into words, seems a contradiction in terms; men have urged it as such; then Christians, lest they should seem to be unduly and harshly insisting upon words which clash with each other, and so should dishonour the truth of God, and cause hearers to stumble, have guarded their words, and explained them; and then for doing this they have been accused of speculating and theorizing. The same result, doubtless, would take place in the Parallel cue already mentioned. Had we no bodies, and were a Revelation made us that there was a race who had bodies as well as souls, what a number of powerful objections should we seem to possess against that Revelation! We might plausibly say, that the words used in conveying it were arbitrary and unmeaning. What (we should ask) was the meaning of saying that the soul had no parts, yet was in every part of the body? what was meant by saying it was every where and no where? how could it be one, and yet repeated, as it were, ten thousand times over in every atom and pore of the body, which it was said to exist in? how could it be confined to the body at all? how did it act upon the body? how happened it, as was pretended, that, when the soul did but will, the arm moved or the feet walked? how can a spirit which cannot touch any thing, yet avail to move so large a mass of matter, and so easily as the human body? These are some of the questions which might be asked, partly on the ground that the alleged fact was impossible, partly that the idea was self-contradictory.

On the distinction between aporias, apparent antinomies and intrinsic impossibilities see also Josef Seifert, *Überwindung des Skandals der reinen Vernunft. Die Widerspruchsfreiheit der Wirklichkeit – trotz Kant* (Freiburg/München: Karl Alber, 2001); "Das Antinomienproblem als ein Grundproblem aller Metaphysik: Kritik der Kritik der reinen Vernunft," *Prima Philosophia* 2 (1989):143–68; *Leib und Seele. Ein Beitrag zur philosophischen Anthropologie* (Salzburg: A. Pustet, 1973).

75 This is a point specifically stressed by Maurice Blondel. See *Internet Encyclopaedia of Philosophy* [http://www.iep.utm.edu/chri1930/], "Christian Philosophy: The 1930s French Debates" which quotes some of the relevant texts by Blondel:
[a] gap coming from above (*Bul. Soc fr. Phil.*, 91)
[the] interior open space or the silence of the soul (*Bul. Soc fr. Phil.*, 91)
infinitesimal and real fissures, 'holes' that require being filled and which admit consequently the presence or even the need of another reality, of a heterogeneous and complementary datum. ("Le problème de la philosophie catholique," 43)

76 We find in Christian thinkers such as Augustine or Thomas Aquinas some purely philosophical works and many other works of combined wisdom of reason and faith. Augustine's *Contra academicos* is possibly the first purely philosophical Book of a Christian, his *De Trinitate, Confessions,* or *De civitate Dei,* on the other hand, combines philosophy, history, theology, and autobiography. Thomas Aquinas' *De Ente et Essentia* is a purely philosophical work, his *Summa Theologica,* and even more Bonaventure's *Commentary on the Sentences of Peter Lombard,* would be Christian philosophical works in the sense we are discussing here.

77 Thus Xenophanes and Plato in *Politeia* 2 reject radically the anthropomorphic and flagrantly evil traits of the Greek gods.

78 I refer here to the dogma of God's universal will to salvation, which makes it virtually necessary to believe that God offered also Pagans a road to salvation in the form of some "baptism of desire" and that philosophers were sent to Greece by God in an analogous way as the Prophets to the Jews, in order to guide them, in a far more modest and inferior way than the prophets, along a road of love of truth and justice that implied a sincere quest for God. This was also the teaching of some of the first philosophers to become Christians, such as Saint Justin the Martyr and Saint Clement of Alexandria.

79 See Friedrich Wilhelm Joseph von Schelling, *Philosophische Untersuchungen über das Wesen der menschlichen Freiheit/Philosophical Investigations into the Essence of Human Freedom,* trans. Jeff Love and Johannes Schmidt (Albany, N.Y.: State University of New York Press, 2006), 61.
. . . the proposition is utterly undeniable: that every-

thing proceeds from the divine nature with absolute
necessity, that everything that is possible by virtue
of this nature must also be actual, and what is not
actual also must be morally impossible.

80   Schelling seeks to deny this objectively logical consequence of his
     position. See Schelling, *ibid.*, 63:

> Hence, what comes from the mere condition or the
> ground, does not come from God, although it is ne-
> cessary from his existence. But it cannot also be said
> that evil comes from the ground or that the will of
> the ground is the originator of evil. For evil can al-
> ways only arise in the innermost will of our own
> heart and is never accomplished without our own
> act.

In spite of his protests, Schelling, like many other philosophers,
arrives at an identification of Good and Evil, both of which would
be rooted in God. See *ibid.*, 63:

> . . . Hence it is entirely correct to say dialectically:
> good and evil are the same thing only seen from dif-
> ferent sides.

81   See Rudolf Otto, *Das Heilige. Über das Irrationale in der Idee des Gött-
     lichen und sein Verhältnis zum Rationalen*, Sonderauflage (Munich:
     Verlag C.H. Beck, 1962)/*The Idea of the Holy. An Inquiry into the
     Non-rational Factor in the Idea of the Divine and Its Relation to the Ra-
     tional*, trans. John W. Harvey, 27th Printing (London/Oxford/New
     York: Oxford University Press, 1982). See the same author, *Aufsätze
     zur Ethik*, ed. Jack Stewart Boozer (München: Beck, 1981). See also
     Max Scheler, "Probleme der Religion," in Max Scheler, *Vom Ewigen
     im Menschen*, 5th ed. (Bern und München: Francke Verlag, 1968),
     101–354; and Dietrich von Hildebrand, *Transformation in Christ. On
     the Christian Attitude of Mind*, last edition with a new sub-title:
     Transformation in Christ. Our Path to Holiness, reprint of 1948 ed.
     (New Hampshire: Sophia Institute Press, 1989).

82   See Giovanni Reale, ed., *Agostino. Amore assoluto e "terza naviga-
     zione"* (Mailand: Rusconi, 1994). See also Josef Seifert, *Essere e per-
     sona. Verso una fondazione fenomenologica di una metafisica classica e
     personalistica* (Milano: Vita e Pensiero, 1989), ch. 5; the same author,
     "Essere Persona Come Perfezione Pura. Il Beato Duns Scoto e una
     nuova metafisica personalistica," De Homine, Dialogo di Filosofia
     11 (Rom: Herder/Università Lateranense, 1994), 57–75, and Josef
     Seifert, "El amor como perfección pura: una metafísica del amor
     como himno filosófico del amor," in *Humanitas, Universidad autó-*

noma del Nuevo León, Anuario del Centro de Estudios Humanísticos,
2004, 65–82.

83 Also all talk of a purgatory, of moral conscience, of the sacraments
of confession and baptism or the annointing of the sick would be
senseless babbling.

84 The third part of the present book is incomparably more extensive
than the corresponding part of the Italian publication *Filosofia cristiana e libertà*. A cura di Gian Paolo Terravecchia. (Brescia: Morcel-
liana, 2013), and was originally published as article (reprinted
here, with small changes, with the kind permission of the Editor
of the *Review of Metaphysics*, Prof. Jude Dougherty): "In Defense
of Free Will: A Critique of Benjamin Libet," *Review of Metaphysics*
65 (2011): 377–407. http://readperiodicals.com/201112/
"2543177011.html; abstract: http://www.reviewofmetaphysics.
org/index.php?option=com_content&view=article&id=66&Ite-
mid=39. Correspondence to: Josef Seifert, Ángel Ganivet 5. 7D, ES
18009 Granada, Granada, Spain, or seifert@institutoifes.es.

85 Benjamin Libet, "Do We Have Free Will?," in *The Oxford Handbook
of Free Will*, ed. Robert Kane (Oxford: Oxford University Press,
2002), 551–64; 551; hereafter DWHFW. The same article is also
reprinted in *Conscious Will and Responsibility*, ed. Walter Sinnott-
Armstrong and Lynn Nadel (New York: Oxford University Press,
2011), 1–10; 1. See also Benjamin Libet, "Time of Conscious Intention to Act in Relation Onset of Cerebral Activity (Readiness Potential): The Unconscious Initiation of a Freely Voluntary Act,"
Brain 106 (1983): 623–42. See also *The Volitional Brain: Towards a
Neuroscience of Free Will*, ed. Benjamin Libet, Anthony Freeman,
and Keith Sutherland (Cambridge, MA: Harvard University Press,
2004); hereafter VB; Benjamin Libet, *Mind Time: The Temporal Factor
in Consciousness* (Boston, Mass. and London: Harvard University
Press, 2004); Benjamin Libet, "Time Factors in Conscious
Processes: Reply to Gilberto Gomes," *Consciousness and Cognition*
9 (2000): 1–12; Benjamin Libet, "Timing of Conscious Experience:
Reply to the 2002 Commentaries on Libet's Findings," *Consciousness and Cognition* 12 (2003): 321–31; Benjamin Libet, "The Timing
of Mental Events: Libet's Experimental Findings and Their Implications," *Consciousness and Cognition* 11 (2002): 291–9. For a solid
philosophical critique of Libet's ideas about timing, see Alfred
Mele, *Effective Intentions: The Power of Conscious Will* (Oxford: Oxford University Press, 2009), 57–59; hereafter EI. See also Benjamin
Libet, "Unconscious Cerebral Initiative and the Role of Conscious
Will in Voluntary Action," *Behavioral and Brain Sciences* 8 (1985):

529; "The Timing of Subjective Experience," *Behavioral and Brain Sciences* 12 (1989): 183.

86   See on this Dietrich von Hildebrand, *What is Philosophy?*, 3rd ed., with an introduction by Josef Seifert (London: Routledge, 1991); Dietrich von Hildebrand, *Che cos'è la filosofia?/What Is Philosophy?* (Milano: Bompiani Testi a fronte, 2001); hereafter WIP; "Das Cogito und die Erkenntnis der realen Welt, Teilveröffentlichung der Salzburger Vorlesungen Hildebrands: 'Wesen und Wert menschlicher Erkenntnis,'" *Aletheia* 6 (1994): 2–27; hererafter *DC*. See likewise Josef Seifert, *Discours des Méthodes. The Methods of Philosophy and Realist Phenomenology*, (Frankfurt / Paris / Ebikon / Lancaster / New Brunswick: Ontos-Verlag, 2009).

87   See Libet, DWHFW. See also Benjamin Libet, "Commentary on 'Free Will in the Light of Neuropsychiatry,'" *Philosophy, Psychiatry, & Psychology* 3, no. 2 (1996): 95–96.

88   Aristotle describes free will when he says, "Therefore it is clear that all the actions of which a man is the first principle and controller may either happen or not happen, and that it depends on himself for them to happen or not, as he is lord over their being and of their non-being. But of those things which it depends on him to do or not to do he is himself the cause, and what he is the cause of is from himself. And since virtue and evilness and the actions that spring from them are in some cases praiseworthy and in other cases blameworthy (for praise and blame are not given to what necessity or fortune or nature determine but to things of which we ourselves are the causes, since for things of which another one is the cause, that person has the blame and the praise), it is clear that both goodness and badness have to do with things of which a man is himself the cause and origin of actions. We must, then, ascertain what is the kind of actions of which a man is himself the cause and origin. Now we all agree that each man is the cause of all those acts that are voluntary and purposive for him individually, and that he is not himself the cause of those that are involuntary. And clearly he commits voluntarily all the acts that he commits purposely. It is clear, then, that both moral virtue and evilness will be in the class of things voluntary." Aristotle, *Eudemian Ethics*, 2.6.8–9; 1223a3 and following (transl. mine): w{ste o{swn pravxewn oJ a[nqrwpovÀ ejstin [5] ajrch; kai; kuvrioÀ, fanero;n o{ti ejndevcetai kai; givnesqai kai; mhv, kai; o{ti ejf jau- Jtw/Ö tauÖt j ejsti givnesqai kai; mhv, w I n ge kuvriovÀ ejsti touÖ ei\nai kai; touÖ mh; ei\nai. o{sa d j ejf j auJtwÖ/ ejsti poieiÖn h] mh; poieiÖn, ai[tioÀ touvtwn aujto;À ejstivn: kai; o{swn ai[tioÀ,

ejf j auJtwÖ/. ejpei; d j h{ te ajreth; kai; hJ kakiva kai; ta; ajp j[10] aujtwÖn e[rga ta; me;n ejpaineta; ta; de; yektav (yevgetai ga;r kai; ejpaineiÖtai ouj dia; ta; ejx ajnavgkhÀ h] tuvchÀ h] fuvsewÀ uJpavrconta, ajll j o{swn aujtoi; ai[tioi ejsmevn: o{swn ga;r a[lloÀ ai[tioÀ, ejkeiÖnoÀ kai; to;n yovgon kai; to;n yovgon kai; to;n e[painon e[cei), dhÖlon o{ti kai; hJ ajreth; kai; hJ kakiva peri; tauÖt j ejstin w l n aujto;À [15] ai[tioÀ kai; ajrch; pravxewn. lhppevon a[ra poivwn aujto;À ai[tioÀ kai; ajrch; pravxewn. pavnteÀ me;n dh; ojmologouÖmen, o{sa me;n ejkouvsia kai; kata; proaivresin th;n eJkavstou, ejkeiÖnon ai[tion ei\nai, o{sa d j ajkouvsia, oujk aujto;n ai[tion. pavnta d j o{sa proelovmenoÀ, kai; ejkw;n dhÖlon o{ti. dhÖlon toivnun o{ti kai; hJ ajreth; kai; hj [20] kakiva twÖn eJkousivwn a]n ei[hsan (Aristotle, *Eudemian Ethics*, ed. F. Susemihl [Leipzig: Teubner, 1884]. Greek online edition in *Perseus*).

In other texts Aristotle calls free will also "the first principle," "the cause" and "the lord of action." See Aristotle, *Magna Moralia*, 87b31 and following, especially 89b6 and following. The moments of self-dominion, self-governance, and self-determination have also been investigated in fine analyses by Karol Wojtyła in his *The Acting Person*, trans. Andrzej Potocki, ed. Anna-Teresa Tymieniecka (Boston: Reidel, 1979).

89 "Libertarian" has, in ordinary language, completely different senses, and its relatively recent philosophical meaning deviates from the ordinary usage of the English or German language and associates quite a few additional elements with the strong defense of free will. For both of these reasons, as a philosophical term, it is an artificial creation. Robert Kane expresses, mainly for the second reason, similar misgivings about the term and proposes to call his "libertarian" position "free willist view." See Robert Kane, *The Significance of Free Will* (Oxford: Oxford University Press, 1998), 3ff. See also the defense of four major positions for and against free will in John Martin Fisher, Robert Kane, Derek Pereboom, and Manuel Vargas, *Four Views on Free Will* (Oxford: Blackwell Publishing, 2007, 2010).

90 Plato has Socrates make the decisive distinction between the *conditions* and *causes* of free acts in *Phaedo* 98b–99d. I have developed some thoughts expressed in this work, particularly on the method of philosophy, the body-mind relation, and freedom and causality, more extensively in Josef Seifert, *Discours des Méthodes. The Methods of Philosophy and Realist Phenomenology* (Frankfurt, Paris, Ebikon, Lancaster, and New Brunswick: Ontos-Verlag, 2009); Josef Seifert, *What is Life? On the Originality, Irreducibility and Value of*

Life, Value Inquiry Book Series, ed. Robert Ginsberg, vol. 51 of the Central European Value Studies, ed. H.G. Callaway (Amsterdam: Rodopi, 1997); and in Josef Seifert, *Überwindung des Skandals der reinen Vernunft. Die Widerspruchsfreiheit der Wirklichkeit–trotz Kant* (Freiburg and München: Karl Alber, 2001).

91 As both Aristotle and Augustine claim.

92 See Augustine, *The City of God*, trans. M. Dods (New York: The Modern Library, 1950), 156–57, chapter 5.10; hereafter CG. See also Kant, *Critique of Pure Reason,* trans. Norman K. Smith (New York: St. Martin's Press, 1965), B 478; hereafter CPR.

93 "Item si quispiam dicat, errare nolo; nonne sive erret sive non erret, errare tamen eum nolle verum erit? Quis est qui huic non impudentissime dicat, Forsitan falleris? cum profecto ubicumque fallatur, falli se tamen nolle non fallitur. Et si hoc scire se dicat, addit quantum vult rerum numerum cognitarum, et numerum esse perspicit infinitum. Qui enim dicit, Nolo me falli et hoc me nolle scio, et hoc me scire scio; jam et si non commoda elocutione, potest hinc infinitum numerum ostendere." Augustine, *De Trinitate*, Corpus Christianorum Series Latina 50A, ed. W.J. Mountain and F. Glorie (Turnhout: Brepols, 1968), chapter 15.12, 21: "Likewise if someone were to say: 'I do not want to err,' will it not be true that whether he errs or does not err, yet he does not want to err? Would it not be the height of impudence of anyone to say to this man: 'Perhaps you are deceived,' since no matter in what he may be deceived, he is certainly not deceived in not willing to be deceived? And if he says that he knows this, he adds as many known things as he pleases, and perceives it to be an infinite number. For he who says, 'I do not want to be deceived, and I know that I do not want this, and I know that I know this,' can also continue from here towards an infinite number, however awkward this manner of expressing it may be" (Augustine, *The Trinity*, trans. Stephen McKenna [slightly modified by me] [Washington, DC: The Catholic University of America Press, 1970], 480–2; hereafter TT).

94 See also the full text of Augustine: "On the other hand, who would doubt that he lives, remembers, understands, wills, thinks, knows, and judges? For even if he doubts, he lives; if he doubts, he remembers why he doubts; if he doubts, he understands that he doubts; if he doubts, he wants [*wills*] to be certain; if he doubts, he thinks; if he doubts, he knows that he does not know; if he doubts, he judges that he ought not to consent rashly. Whoever then doubts about anything else ought never to doubt about all of

these; for if they were not, he would be unable to doubt about anything at all" (Augustine, TT, 480–82). "Vivere se tamen et meminisse, et intelligere, et velle, et cogitare, et scire, et judicare quis dubitet? Quandoquidem etiam si dubitat, vivit; si dubitat, unde dubitet, meminit; si dubitat, dubitare se intelligit; si dubitat, certus esse vult; si dubitat, cogitat; si dubitat, scit se nescire; si dubitat, judicat non se temere consentire oportere. Quisquis igitur aliunde dubitat, de his omnibus dubitare non debet: quae si non essent, de ulla re dubitare non posset." René Descartes gains the same insight as Augustine, as Sophie Berman well explains, citing a short text of his: "[I]t [the free will] cannot be forced by any external power to choose what it does not want. That we possess such freedom of choice, he [Descartes] says, 'is so evident that it must be counted among the first and most common notions. . . .'" See her article: "Human Freedom in Anselm and Descartes," *Saint Anselm Journal* 2 (2004): 5. René Descartes, *Principles of Philosophy* I, 39; in René Descartes, *The Philosophical Works*, trans. E.S. Haldane and G.R.T. Ross (New York: Dover Publications, 1955), 1:205–6. The text, putting this insight into the extremely misleading language of the "inborn ideas" continues: "that are innate in us" (ibid., 206).

95   See, likewise, Hans Urs von Balthasar, *Theodramatik*, vol. 2 (Einsiedeln: Johannes Verlag, 1976): *Die Personen des Spiels, 1: Der Mensch in Gott*, 186–90. See also Balthasar, *TheoLogik, Wahrheit der Welt* (Einsiedeln: Johannes Verlag, 1985), vol. II, A., *Wahrheit als Freiheit*, 1. See also Hans-Eduard Hengstenberg, *Grundlegung der Ethik* (Stuttgart: Kohlhammer, 1969), 11–15; hereafter *GE*, where he analyzes a similar ineluctable givenness of moral good and evil, a sort of cogito-argument for the givenness of good and evil.

96   This has been called in German *Vollzugsbewußtsein*. See, on this notion of *Vollzugsbewußtsein*, Dietrich von Hildebrand, *Die Idee der sittlichen Handlung*, 2nd ed. (Darmstadt: Wissenschaftliche Buchgesellschaft, 1969), 8–12; Dietrich von Hildebrand, *Moralia*, Nachgelassenes Werk, Gesammelte Werke, Band V (Regensburg: Josef Habbel, 1980), 208–10; hereafter *MOR*; Dietrich von Hildebrand, *Ästhetik*, vol. 1, Gesammelte Werke (Stuttgart: Kohlhammer, 1977), 32–40, 49–57; Dietrich von Hildebrand, *Ethik* (Stuttgart: Kohlhammer, Stuttgart, 1971), 202–4, 212, 242; Dietrich von Hildebrand, *Ethics*, 2nd ed. (Chicago: Franciscan Herald Press, 1978), 191–5; hereafter *ES*; Hildebrand, *DC*; Dietrich von Hildebrand, *Transformation in Christ. Our Path to Holiness* (New Hampshire: Sophia Institute Press. 1989), chapter 4; *Die Umgestaltung in Christus. Über christliche Grundhaltung*, 5th ed., Gesammelte Werke, vol. 10 (Regensburg: Habbel, 1971), chapter 4. See also the first

part of Karol Wojtyła, *The Acting Person* (Boston: Reidel, 1979); see also the corrected text, authorized by the author (unpublished), Library of the International Academy of Philosophy in the Principality Liechtenstein, Bendern; hereafter *AP*.

97 See Karol Wojtyła, *AP*, 10–15.

98 See René Descartes, *Meditationes de Prima Philosophia*, vol. 7 of *Oeuvres de Descartes*, ed. Charles Adam and Paul Tannery (Paris: J. Vrin, 1983), Meditation 4.

99 See Ludger Hölscher, *The Reality of the Mind. St. Augustine's Arguments for the Human Soul as Spiritual Substance* (London: Routledge and Kegan Paul, 1986).

100 As expressed by Saint Augustine in a way quite similar to Aristotle's formulation: "for we do many things which, if we were not willing, we should certainly not do. This is primarily true of the act of willing itself—for if we will, it *is;* if we will not, it *is* not." Augustine continues a little further down: "Our wills, therefore, *exist* as *wills,* and do themselves whatever we do by willing, and which would not be done if we were unwilling." See Augustine, *CG,* 5.10, 156–57 (emphasis mine). Kant, too, when he expresses the profound puzzle of such an absolute beginning of causality in free will, refers to this relationship—mentioned by Plato—between the essence of free will and a first mover. Kant, *CPR,* B 478.

101 See the above quotes of Augustine. See, also D. von Hildebrand, *DC,* 2–27.

102 Daniel M. Wegner, *The Illusion of Conscious Free Will* (Cambridge, Mass.: MIT Press, 2002); hereafter *IFW*.

103 Viktor E. Frankl has insisted on this in most of his many books and articles. For a presentation of the central role of this insight into human free will and responsibility for logotherapy, see Elisabeth Lukas, *Lehrbuch der Logotherapie. Menschenbild und Methoden* (München and Wien: Profil, 1997). See also Viktor E. Frankl, *Sinn als anthropologische Kategorie: Meaning as an Anthropological Category* (Heidelberg: Universitätsverlag C. Winter, 1996), 19–29.

104 As they have been analyzed by Scheler in Max Scheler, "Idole der Selbsterkenntnis," in vol. 5 of *Gesammelte Werke*, ed. Manfred Frings (Bern and München: Francke Verlag, 1968), translated as "The Idols of Self-Knowledge," in *Selected Philosophical Essays,* trans. David Lachterman (Evanston, IL: Northwestern University Press, 1973); hereafter ISE. A psychologist who has attacked free will on these grounds of self-deceptions is Daniel M. Wegner, *IFW.*

105 See Balduin Schwarz, *Das Problem des Irrtums in der Philosophie*

(Münster, Aschaffenburg, 1934).

106 "Why, then, does truth generate hatred, and why does thy servant who preaches the truth come to be an enemy to them who also love the happy life, which is nothing else than joy in the truth—unless it be that truth is loved in such a way that those who love something else besides her wish that to be the truth which they do love. Since they are unwilling to be deceived, they are unwilling to be convinced that they have been deceived. Therefore, they hate the truth for the sake of whatever it is that they love in place of the truth. They love truth when she shines on them; and hate her when she rebukes them. And since they are not willing to be deceived, but do wish to deceive, they love truth when she reveals herself and hate her when she reveals them. On this account, she will so repay them that those who are unwilling to be exposed by her she will indeed expose against their will, and yet will not disclose herself to them. . . . Thus, thus, truly thus: the human mind so blind and sick, so base and ill-mannered, desires to lie hidden, but does not wish that anything should be hidden from it. And yet the opposite is what happens— the mind itself is not hidden from the truth, but the truth is hidden from it. Yet even so, for all its wretchedness, it still prefers to rejoice in truth rather than in known falsehoods. It will, then, be happy only when without other distractions it comes to rejoice in that single Truth through which all things else are true." Augustine, *Confessions*, in *Confessions and Enchiridion*, trans. and ed. Albert C. Outler, Library of Christian Classics, vol. 7 (Philadelphia: Westminster Press, 1955), Book X, 34.

107 An extremely important advantage of the Augustinian over the Cartesian *Cogito* lies in Augustine's clear grasp of this fact, which is contradicted by certain passages in René Descartes, *Discours de la Methode*, in *Oeuvres de Descartes*, 6:1–78, and in his letters to Mersenne, in which he claims that God's omnipotence could change all truths such that there are, according to him, no truly eternal and absolutely necessary truths. See Jean-Luc Marion, *Sur la théologie blanche de Descartes* (Paris: Presses Universitaires de France, 1981); Jean-Luc Marion, *Sur l'ontologie grise de Descartes. Savoir aristotélicien et science cartésienne dans les Regulae*, 2nd ed. (Paris: J. Vrin, 1981).

108 The scholastics expressed this necessary truth by saying *nil volitum nisi cogitatum* (nothing is willed if it is not thought), and: *Nil volitum nisi (prae)cognitum* (nothing is willed that is not first known).

109 We owe a thorough development of these distinctions to Dietrich von Hildebrand, *ES*, chapters 1–7, 17–25.

110 On this third way to know free will, Kant has insisted much, even though he profoundly misinterpreted his insight in a subjectivist way. See, for example Immanuel Kant, *Kritik der praktischen Vernunft* (1788), in *Kants Werke*, Akademie-Textausgabe (Berlin: Walter de Gruyter & Co., 1968), § 6, pp. 5, 29–30.

111 On the interpretation of an ought as rooted in the call to give a due value response to a good endowed with intrinsic value, see Dietrich von Hildebrand, *ES*, ch. 1–3; 17–18. Hildebrand has shown that this is the deepest source of any ought: to give a good endowed with intrinsic values a response due to it.

112 To refute this objection, we must refer the reader to other works in ethics, for example, Hildebrand, *ES*, chapter 9, where many forms of ethical relativism are refuted, or Max Scheler's distinction between objective values and subjective value-illusions in his masterwork, *Das Ressentiment im Aufbau der Moralen*, in *Vom Umsturz der Werte* (Bern-München: Francke-Verlag, 1955). It was translated as *Ressentiment*, trans. William W Holdheim, edited with an introduction by Lewis A. Coser (New York: Free Press of Glencoe, 1961; New York: Schocken Books, 1972).

113 On this, see the outstanding chapter 25 on "cooperative freedom" in Hildebrand, *ES*. There are also other sources of an ought, for example, freely entered commitments, promises, and so on. See Dietrich von Hildebrand, *MOR*.

114 An excellent form of this kind of objectivist "transcendental argument" for free will and against determinism we owe to Hans Jonas. In his book *Macht oder Ohnmacht der Subjektivität? Das Leib-Seele-Problem im Vorfeld des Prinzips Verantwortung* (Frankfurt: A.M., 1981); hereafter LSPVV. He refutes brilliantly the materialist ontology and the deterministic account of the mind, regrettably without rejecting explicitly the kind of biologistic monism defended in some of his earlier essays collected in Hans Jonas, *The Phenomenon of Life. Toward a Philosophical Biology* (New York: Harper and Row, 1966; New York: Dell Publishing Co., 1968; Evanston, Ill.: Northwestern University Press, 2001); hereafter *PL*. Jonas opens his book by relating the historical fact that we report in the text.

115 See on such undeniable truths (*verità innegabili*) also Giovanni Reale, *Storia della filosofía antica*, 5 vols., 10th ed. (Milan: Vita e Pensiero, 1995), volume 2.

116 Jonas shows this excellently in LSPVV.

117 See also the impressive version of this objectivist transcendental argument in the introductory pages of Hans-Eduard Hengstenberg, *GE*. A similar analysis of the presupposedness of free will in the sim-

plest everyday experiences is found in John R. Searle, *Freedom and Neurobiology: Reflections on Free Will, Language, and Political Power* (New York: Columbia University Press, 2007), 43; hereafter FN.

118 See Max Scheler, "Reue und Wiedergeburt," in *Vom Ewigen im Menschen*, 5th ed., ed. Maria Scheler (Bern and München: Francke Verlag, 1968), 27–59; see also Max Scheler, *Selected Philosophical Essays*, trans. and introduction by David Lachterman (Evanston, IL: Northwestern University Press, 1973). See likewise Josef Seifert, "Scheler on Repentance", in: John F. Crosby, (Ed.), *Max Scheler, American Catholic Philosophical Quarterly*, 79, 1 (Winter 2005), 183–202.

119 See Seneca, *Moral Essays*, Volume III, Loeb Classical Library 310, *De Beneficiis*, III.xvii.3–4. See also Seneca, *De Beneficiis*, III.xix.1: "Beneficium enim id est, quod quis dedit, cum illi liceret et non dare." ("A benefit is what someone gave when he was free and allowed not to give it," transl. mine).

120 See Balduin Schwarz, "Über die Dankbarkeit," in *Wirklichkeit der Mitte. Beiträge zu einer Strukturanthropologie. Festgabe für August Vetter zum 80. Geburtstag*, ed. J. Tenzler (Freiburg-München, 1968), 677–704; Balduin Schwarz, "Del agradecimiento," in *Ediciones del Departamento de Etica y Sociologia de la Universidad Complutense en homenaje a su catedrático director R.P. José Todolí Duque O.P. con ocasion de su jubilación*, trans. Juan Miguel Palacios (Madrid: May 27, 1985); Balduin Schwarz, "Der Dank als Gesinnung und Tat," in *Danken und Dankbarkeit. Eine universale Dimension des Menschseins*, ed. Josef Seifert (Heidelberg: Carl Winter-Universitätverlag, 1992), 15–26; Balduin Schwarz, "Some reflections on gratitude," in *The Human Person and the World of Values: A Tribute to Dietrich von Hildebrand by his Friends in Philosophy* (New York: Fordham University Press, 1960; reprinted Westport, Connecticut: Greenwood Press Publishers, 1972), 168–191; Balduin Schwarz, "Réflexions sur la gratitude et l'admiration," in *Entretiens autour de Gabriel Marcel* (Neuchâtel, 1976), 229–48, and 242–48, discussion. See also *Dankbarkeit ist das Gedächtnis des Herzens. Aphorismen*, ed. Balduin Schwarz (München: Don Bosco Verlag, 1992).

121 See Scheler, ISE.

122 See Edith Stein, *Zum Problem der Einfühlung*, (Halle A.D.S.: Buchdruckerei des Waisenhauses, 1917; reprint, München: Kaffke, 1980). See also Mariano Crespo, *Phänomenologie des Verzeihens* (Heidelberg: Universitätsverlag C. Winter, 2002), and Mariano Crespo, *El perdón, Una investigación filosófica* (Madrid: Ediciones Encuentro, 2004).

123 Augustine, as well as Kant and Roman Ingarden argue that way. See Augustine, the quoted texts above, and particularly in *De civitate Dei*, in Corpus Christianorum Series Latina 47–48, ed. B. Dombart and A. Kalb (Turnhout: Brepols, 1955), Book 5, 9–11. See also Immanuel Kant who presents, in the *thesis* of the third antinomy, an excellent argument for the necessary presupposedness of free will for efficient causality, while he construes in the antithesis of the third antinomy an alleged contradiction between causality and freedom, which he uses as main or only proof for his Copernican turn because he believes that this and similar contradictions cannot be resolved on the basis of a realist philosophy that takes freedom and causality, and other things, as "things in themselves." See Immanuel Kant, "The Antinomy of Pure Reason," in *CPR; Kritik der reinen Vernunft*, in vol. 3 of *Kants Werke*, Akademie-Textausgabe (Berlin: Walter de Gruyter & Co., 1968), B 472–79; see also B 472–79, 558–62; 433–54; especially B 448–49. See likewise on the perfect harmony between causality and free will Roman Ingarden, *Von der Verantwortung. Ihre ontischen Fundamente* (Stuttgart: Philipp Reclam, 1970).

124 In a fuller account of this argument, one would have to consider the objections from an alleged "causally closed universe" and Kant's and others' objection that there is an antinomy here because causality and the law of causality and of sufficient reason both presuppose and contradict free will.

125 Likewise, the evil decision of the greedy man *not to give an honest and truly poor beggar* some alms is not a mere lack of acting (a pure absence of giving something to him) but a *free decision not to give*. Hence, as free act, it is as "positively" a free act as giving alms.

126 See Karl R. Popper and John C. Eccles, *The Self and Its Brain* (Berlin, Heidelberg, London, and New York: Springer-Verlag International, 1977; corrected printing, 1981). Josef Seifert, *Überwindung des Skandals der reinen Vernunft. Die Widerspruchsfreiheit der Wirklichkeit – trotz Kant*, (Freiburg / München: Karl Alber, 2001); *Superación del escándalo de la razón pura. La ausencia de contradicción de la realidad, a pesar de Kant*. Biblioteca filosófica "El Carro Alado". Traducción Rogelio Rovira. (Madrid: Ediciones Cristianidad, 2007); see also Josef Seifert: "Das Antinomienproblem als ein Grundproblem aller Metaphysik: Kritik der Kritik der reinen Vernunft" in Prima Philosophia, Bd. 2, H 2, 1989: El problema de las antinomias considerado como un problema fundamental de toda Metafisica: Critica de la 'Critica de la Razón Pura'", *Revista de Filosofía* 3. epoca, vol 6 (1993); traducción de Rogelio Rovira, pp. 89–117;

"Persons and Causes: beyond Aristotle," *Journal of East-West Thought*, Fall Issue Nr. 3 Vol. 2, September 2012, pp. 1–32; the same author, "Can Neurological Evidence Refute Free Will? The Failure of a Phenomenological Analysis of Acts in Libet's Denial of 'Positive Free Will'", *Pensamiento. Revista de investigación e información filosófica*, vol. 67, núm. 254, *Ciencia, filosofía y religion. Serie especial no 5* (2011), 1077–1098.

127 This agument I have developed much more in J. Seifert, "Can Neurological Evidence Refute Free Will? The Failure of a Phenomenological Analysis of Acts in Libet's Denial of 'Positive Free Will'", *Pensamiento. Revista de investigación e información filosófica*, vol. 67, núm. 254, *Ciencia, filosofía y religion. Serie especial no 5* (2011), 1077–1098.

128 Also, unfree life belongs to such forces extrinsic to a closed material universe. See Hans Jonas, *PL*; Hans Jonas, LSPVV.

INDEX